"The call to courage ripples through the classroom, neighborhoods, boardrooms, and church pews. If we are to model a compelling, God-honoring, and biblical life, we have no choice but to risk. You'll be motivated while you are convicted, encouraged while you are moved, and grounded while you are active."

— DANIEL S. WOLGEMUTH, president,
Youth for Christ, USA

"*When God Says Jump* encapsulates not only the passion but also the principles required of Jesus-followers to become fully engaged in their faith. Briggs' daring call will likely leave you uncomfortable in your status quo, but his faith-centered challenge will also have you salivating for the thrill that comes in risking everything for the Creator. In a time where many seem to be at ease in their faith, Briggs jumps into his with such fervor, you'll wonder what the heck you're doing still in the plane."

— MATTHEW PAUL TURNER, author of
Provocative Faith: Walking Away from Ordinary and *Everything
You Need to Know Before College*

"J.R. Briggs challenges all ages to courageously discard the 'be safe' life in favor of something more: the risk that ultimately accompanies a truly fulfilled life that trusts God and loosens the grip of fear and control. J.R.'s call to his generation is summed up by the words from a Disney movie, 'The brave may not live forever but the cautious do not live at all.'"

— SIBYL TOWNER , director of spiritual mentoring,
Willow Creek Community Church

"So often in our walk with Christ, we expect the Lord's directions and His will to be crystal clear, complete with detailed explanations that make perfect sense to us. But sometimes God just says, 'Jump.' J.R. Briggs offers compelling and solid biblical examples for us to pattern our lives after, men and women who weren't afraid to jump and whose lives were never the same because of this kind of life-changing trust. J.R. has convinced *me* to jump; are *you* brave enough to take that call?"

— DAVE DRAVECKY, president, Dave Dravecky's Outreach of Hope

"For Christians living in a culture touting comfort and security at any cost, complacency is a lurking danger. The Bible repeatedly calls us to embrace the unknown. J.R. Briggs offers a timely message to leave safety behind, follow Jesus, and engage in a life of adventure with the God of the universe."

— AARON STERN, college/twentysomethings pastor, New Life Church

"Taking risks for God involves faith and often sacrifice. J.R. Briggs lives a life that models trusting God for big things. He walks the talk!"

— TOM YEAKLEY, leader development specialist, The Navigators

"With fresh takes on the likes of Abraham, Mary, Jeremiah, and even Rosa Parks, Briggs issues an invitation to us all: 'Cash in your fears of losing control, of failure, of appearing vulnerable, and of facing hardship for the just-jump life Christ offers.' The watching world awaits. Are you in?"

— ASHLEY WIERSMA, freelance writer;
coauthor of *Marked for Life*

"A beautiful portrayal of the raw and difficult aspects of faith. And J.R. is no theoretician. He's a practitioner, a pioneer, and a pilgrim. You will enjoy and be challenged by this very readable story."

— JASON MALEC, MA.Th., director,
Starting Point, www.startingpoint.com

"J.R. Briggs does not disappoint as he invites—no, dares—his readers to consider the theological significance of risk taking. J.R. suggests that doing the unimagined and the not-always-planned honors the God who made us. He reminds us that boredom is neither our calling nor that of the people whose stories dot the Scriptures. A great read!"

— RICHARD ALLEN FARMER, Bible expositor;
concert artist; former campus pastor,
Taylor University and Gordon College

J.R. BRIGGS

WHEN GOD SAYS JUMP

BIBLICAL STORIES THAT INSPIRE YOU TO RISK BIG

TH1NK Books
an imprint of NavPress®

TH1NK
P.O. Box 35001
Colorado Springs, Colorado 80935

TH1NK is an imprint of NavPress.
TH1NK and the TH1NK logo are registered trademarks of NavPress. Absence of ® in connection with marks of NavPress or other parties does not indicate an absence of registration of those marks.

ISBN 1-57683-859-5

Cover design by Mattson Creative
Cover photo by Getty Images/Hulton Archive
Creative Team: Nicci Hubert, Arvid Wallen, Cara Iverson, Bob Bubnis

Some of the anecdotal illustrations in this book are true to life and are included with the permission of the persons involved. All other illustrations are composites of real situations, and any resemblance to people living or dead is coincidental.

Unless otherwise identified, all Scripture quotations in this publication are taken from the HOLY BIBLE: NEW INTERNATIONAL VERSION® (NIV®). Copyright © 1973, 1978, 1984 by International Bible Society. Used by permission of Zondervan Publishing House. All rights reserved. Other versions used include: *THE MESSAGE* (MSG). Copyright © 1993, 1994, 1995, 1996, 2000, 2001, 2002. Used by permission of NavPress Publishing Group; the *Holy Bible, New Living Translation* (NLT), copyright © 1996. Used by permission of Tyndale House Publishers, Inc., Wheaton, Illinois 60189. All rights reserved; and the *New King James Version* (NKJV). Copyright © 1982 by Thomas Nelson, Inc. Used by permission. All rights reserved.

Briggs, J. R., 1979-
    When God says jump : biblical stories that inspire you to risk big /
J.R. Briggs.
        p. cm.
    Includes bibliographical references.
    ISBN 1-57683-859-5
    1. Christian youth--Religious life. 2. Risk taking
(Psychology)--Religious aspects--Christianity. 3. Obedience--Religious
aspects--Christianity. 4. Risk taking (Psychology)--Biblical teaching.
5. Obedience--Biblical teaching. I. Title.
    BV4531.3.B75 2006
    2005027001

Printed in the United States of America

2 3 4 5 6 7 8 9 10 / 10 09 08 07 06

To Megan, who risked big when she
committed to doing life with me

Risk

To laugh is to risk appearing the fool
To weep is to risk appearing sentimental
To reach out to others is to risk involvement
To expose feelings is to risk exposing your true self
To place your ideas, your dreams before a crowd
 is to risk their loss
To love is to risk not being loved in return
To live is to risk dying
To hope is to risk despair
To try is to risk failure
But risks must be taken,
 because the greatest hazard in life is to do nothing.
The person who risks nothing,
 does nothing, has nothing, and is nothing.
He may avoid suffering and sorrow,
 but he cannot learn, feel, change, grow, love, live.
Chained by his attitudes, he is a slave,
 he forfeited his freedom.
Only the person who risks can be free.

—Author Unknown

Contents

Acknowledgments

It takes a village to craft a good sermon, the old adage goes. Writing a book is no different. There are many people I wish to thank for making this book possible.

I'm extremely grateful for my wife, Megan, who put up with me when I was not fun to be around. She cooked numerous dinners, brought me cups of tea in the basement, kissed me on the forehead, and told me how proud she was of me. Without her support, patience, and encouragement, I would have given up on this project long ago.

A special thanks to the community of faith at Pierced, the guinea pigs for this original concept in the summer of 2004. You have taught Megan and me more than we could ever teach you. You are truly a privilege to serve with.

Andrew Hess, Christian Hill, Stuart Davis, Rick and Cindi Holman, Dave and Debbie Briggs, Josh Devlin, Tom Smith, Chris Stroup, and Matt Braham read early editions of the manuscript, offered honest feedback, and engaged in conversation that helped steer this concept in the direction it deserved.

Dave Dravecky, Don Miller, and Lauren Winner encouraged me on my trek through the rugged wilderness of First-Time-Author Land.

My brother, Alan, who transcribed large portions of the manuscript, helped me think more critically about risk in the Christian life and sculpt those thoughts into a coherent message.

Thanks to J. H. for the extra motivation.

I am deeply grateful to my editor, Nicci Hubert, a dear friend to Megan and me, who believed in this project long before I ever did. She has been a counselor and cheerleader from start to finish. She went well beyond the call of duty in her editorial role on this project.

And finally, thanks to the many friends at NavPress for their balance of professionalism and a personal touch. I never thought in a million years I would be on the other side of this process. It's been a joy partnering with you again.

The dangers of life are infinite, and among them is safety.

— Goethe

Courage is not limited to the battlefield or the Indianapolis 500 or bravely catching a thief in your house. The real tests of courage are much quieter. They are the inner tests, like remaining faithful when nobody's looking, like enduring pain when the room is empty, like standing alone when you're misunderstood.

— Charles Swindoll

risk *n.* 1. exposure to loss or harm; danger; peril. 2. change; hazard. 3. a contingency covered by insurance. 4. a chance of suffering or encountering harm or loss.

v. 1. expose to injury or loss. 2. take the chance of.

risky *adj.*

WHAT'S THE RISK?

AN INTRODUCTION TO THE LIFE YOU COULD BE LIVING

he conversation still haunts me. Although it happened a few years ago, I still remember it as though it were yesterday. As I waited for a friend to meet me for teriyaki steak and rice bowls at Samurai Sam's, I struck up a conversation with a man probably in his fifties who worked for a large, internationally known corporation just down the street. After some small talk, I asked the man what he did for a living. He told me he had been an accountant for over thirty years.

"Thirty years," I said. "You must love accounting."

Once I said that, his demeanor changed. His head fell, and a mix of embarrassment and shame spread across his face. His response surprised me.

"Actually, I hate it."

"In all due respect," I asked him, "if you hate it, why do you still do it after three decades?"

I could tell the man was uncomfortable, because he could only stare at the floor as though the answer could somehow be located on his shoes. Awkward silence followed, and I wondered if I should have even asked the question in the first place. Finally, he spoke, and his response startled me with its simplicity: "Well, it was just the safe thing to do."

His company and other U.S. companies had offered him various jobs — attractive and exciting jobs, he told me—but they would have involved working with a new set of coworkers, changing companies, or moving his family to a different city to start over. The safe, comfortable response was to just continue doing what he was doing. It was secure. His accounting job was "good enough" for him—and he hated it.

When my friend eventually showed up, I waved a warm good-bye to the accountant. My friend and I enjoyed our lunch, but I just could not shake the conversation I had with the accountant. I walked out of Samurai Sam's that day promising myself I would never work in a job if I harbored those empty feelings. I didn't want to live a life of regret.

14

A few months later, I remembered this accountant and wondered, *What if that were me?* As I thought about it more, I realized something terrifying: Much of the time, I *am* that accountant. I pull that stunt all the time. It may not be with my job, but I play it safe on a regular basis. I bask in the glory of my security and hold on tightly to the areas of my life I can control. I have an allergic reaction to risking anything remotely important to me.

At a recent conference, church consultant Reggie McNeal said, "Most ministry decisions are made as a result of two factors: fear and control."[1] What a simple and profound thought. After spending some time chewing on this, I concluded that while I agree with him, I think it's even broader: I think most decisions we make in our *lives* are because of fear and control. I think what makes risk so difficult is that when we risk something, we are no longer in complete control and it freaks us out. We all know that we crave control. We crave it more than a pregnant woman craves pickles and mint chocolate chip ice cream at 2 a.m. And just like the pregnant woman's cravings control her poor husband, our desires for control can easily control us. When we feel as if we have control over a person or situation or reputation or results, we feel safe and secure. The more control we possess, the fewer opportunities we find for risk, and the more we believe *fear* and *lack of control* and *risk* are bad words.

The Rampant Effect of Boredom

We've all been asked at parties, "What are your favorite movies?" To that question, I often answer, *"Shrek."* I know, it's probably not what you would expect a twenty-six-year-old pastor to claim as a favorite, but there you go. I love it. It's hilarious. I especially like Eddie Murphy as the mouthy, arrogant, tactless donkey who can't shut up to save his life. In one of my favorite scenes, the big green ogre travels to rescue Princess Fiona, while Donkey tags along annoying the snot out of him. While Princess Fiona is trapped in a castle surrounded by boiling lava, Shrek and Donkey cross a wobbly, unstable bridge, and Donkey, out of fear, wants to turn around. In great trepidation, Donkey yells, "I'm not going!" to which Shrek replies, "You're already halfway." And Donkey responds, "Yeah, but I know *that* half is safe!" pointing toward land where they had just come from. Many times I walk through life on the safe half of the bridge. It's as if I shout, "Yeah, but I know *that* half of my life is safe!" As they say, hindsight is 20/20, and I know what decisions in my past were good or bad. So, if I follow the pattern of retracing my steps, I should be just fine. And it's my hunch that I'm not the only one who thinks this way. If you look at your own life, you might find a little bit of Donkey in yourself.

What does it take to cross the second half of the bridge? I think it's courage. I've heard it said that courage is the most important of

15

all virtues, the very foundation of all other virtues. In theory, risk and courage sound good, but when the opportunity to risk presents itself, we wonder if it's really worth all the time and effort when so much is at stake. It's when theory shifts to practice that I have so much trouble because I lack the courage to take the risk. Talking about risk, learning about it, and even reading about it are all fun. It's when I'm truly faced with risking something that it becomes hard for me.

When we, especially guys, think about courage, we often recall *Braveheart*. We see William Wallace, played by Mel Gibson, as the ultimate brave man who fights for his love, his country, and his life with the courage of a bear, and it makes us want to be like him. But back in our real lives when we're in a circumstance in which courage is required, we have anything *but* brave hearts. We lack brave hearts because we are afraid. We're afraid of losing control, we're afraid of failure, we're afraid of putting ourselves out there, being vulnerable, and facing any kind of hardship. Life is better when it's easy, right?

But a big problem with living an easy, risk-free life is that we get bored — quickly. It seems the reason the comic strip *Dilbert* is so popular and the movie *Office Space* remains a cult-classic is that Americans can relate to them a great deal. Cubicles at work and cookie-cutter houses in the suburbs give people a vanilla life, a life we're all pretty used to and sick of, but we're afraid to try new flavors. No wonder people live for the weekends and dread Monday mornings at the office. The status-quo life is bland, and we know it. But we're so paralyzed by failure that we settle and merely exist. In his book *Wild at Heart*, John Eldredge accurately points out that most men act like they are here on earth to simply kill time — and it's killing them.[2] I think this is true not only for men but for Americans in general.

Life Is Not a Risk-Free Trial Offer

Our lives were not meant to be easy and risk-free. When I think of "risk-free," I often think of those racing games at the arcade. I pop in two quarters and get ninety seconds of surreality behind the wheel on the oval track. You can almost smell the burnt rubber. In the blink of an eye, I make a sharp move, scrape against the car beside me, flip over, and am engulfed in flames. Then those two little words flash across the screen: "Game Over." Dang. But the good news is, all I have to do is simply reach in my pocket for two more quarters and press "Continue."

We all know that when we finish here on earth and the words "Game Over" flash across our screen, there will be no opportunity to reach for two more quarters and press "Continue." How we spend our days is precious, full of eternal significance and potential. As the band Switchfoot sings, "We were meant to live for so much more." We have a decision to make: waste our lives in safety and predictability, or milk this life for all it's worth. And if we choose a safe life, we are ironically risking the most: We are choosing not to live at all.

17

Risky, but Not Reckless

Right now you might be thinking, *There's gotta be a limit to taking risks. There's a balance, right?* Well, yeah. We don't just jump off of skyscrapers in the spur of the moment and rationalize it by saying, "Hey, I felt God calling me to take risks." Nor would we withhold our final English essay from our professor because we wanted to stop being so afraid of failure. Most of us wouldn't intentionally put ourselves in harm's way only to end up in the hospital with four broken ribs or hypothermia or a concussion or a ruptured spleen just for the thrill of it, because we know pretty quickly that's not God's version of risk. Risk is not some free ticket to participate in foolish stunts and self-inflicted pain. There's a difference between obeying God's call to relinquish control to Him and intentionally messing up our future. The latter is not risk taking—it's just being an idiot (see Ephesians 5:15).

Lots of people take risk too far, some further than others. In an article called "The Arrogance of Risk," John Fry explores the issue of people embracing risk but ignoring responsibility. To him, this behavior equals selfishness, a symptom of the "me generation." Bruce Tremper, director of the Utah Avalanche Center, said, "We've got people actually trying to cause avalanches."[3] It's this type of stuff that, Fry says, has given birth to a new sport: "the intersection of risk and stupidity."[4]

There is a balance, indeed, and knowing that balance comes from wisdom and discernment. Over the past few months, I've learned to pray a new prayer: "God, give me courage and wisdom today." I don't want to live a life without courage, and I certainly don't want to live a life of zeal and be stupid about it. Asking the Holy Spirit to direct you with the proper balance of courage and wisdom, I believe, will open your eyes to the opportunities to risk that God brings on a regular basis.

Where's Our Example?

Let's try a little exercise. Try to name five people you know whom you would describe as true risk takers. Having a hard time? Me, too. I've been thinking about this for about six months now and can come up with only three. Other than movie characters (of which there are numerous examples) and heroic figures such as America's soldiers in Iraq and the 9/11 firefighters and police officers, I'm scraping to come up with people who would fit the description of courageous living.[5] Maybe that's telling me I don't know the true definition of a risk taker, so I wouldn't know how or where to find such a person. Or maybe I know more risk takers than I think, but they're so busy risking big for God that they don't have time to explain it to me. But perhaps the fact I can say I know only three risk takers says something else: Maybe it implies that many of us are not truly following God because we're not taking risks.

I am, to be sure, no expert at this risk thing (a fact that has made writing this book more difficult than I had imagined). As I began to write, I understood there was a deep need for us as followers of Jesus to live courageously, but I was knocked off my rocker to find a huge void in my own life. Nonetheless, this isn't just *my* problem: I have observed that all around me there is a great absence of people who are engaging in risk-filled living.

So, how do we know where to start, how to risk, what to risk? Some would say we can find our examples from our culture, but it seems our culture often speaks out of two sides of its mouth. Think about it: Our culture says risk is attractive, noble, even sexy. How else are you going to get the girl or make loads of money or get to the bottom of that double-black diamond on your snowboard? Risk pumps adrenaline through your veins and makes life much more thrilling. Life, culture tells us, would be boring without it. Yet at the very same time, our culture tells us to play it safe, not take chances, and take the path of safety and security. That's why when you were a kid, your mom probably never kissed you on the forehead and said, "Now go and live dangerously and take some risks," as you dashed off to your friend Billy's house to play. Instead, she probably said two motherly words of wisdom: *Be safe.*

And as we grow up, we take the safe path: enroll in the right college to get a good education to land a well-paying job, settle down, get married, have kids, and go on nice vacations. It's the American dream! And while there's nothing wrong with a good education or a high-paying job, those things don't guarantee a full life of purpose and meaning and significance. Certainly, our culture has caused us quite a bit of confusion.

As Christ followers, we're called to live lives that are anything *but* risk-free. We're called to lives of adventure—heart-pumping, life-altering, category-shattering endangerment—in following the Great Risk Taker Himself. Jesus didn't fit into anybody's categories. Nobody could slap a label on Him, and that's because He didn't care if people didn't like Him or if His life were on the line. He challenged the religious and the irreligious. He comforted the disturbed and disturbed the comfortable. He spoke truth that ticked people off. Jesus ripped people's security blankets in two—not to be a jerk but to expose people to the idea of life, real life, which was His purpose for coming to earth in the first place. And He paid the price that no man or woman in the history of the world could, or would, by climbing up a wooden execution device and spreading out His arms.

Christians, and non-Christians too, often think of Jesus as a really nice (and wimpy) guy who walked around the earth, incapable of having fun or raising His voice under any circumstance. Philip Yancey has said that even our pictures and paintings of Jesus are sterilized and lack any kind of personality. Yancey wrote, "How would telling people to be nice to one another get a man crucified? What government would execute Mister Rogers or Captain Kangaroo?"[6] And while Jesus encouraged us to love our neighbors, He probably didn't sing a song about them in a red sweater while chatting with small hand puppets. But much of the time, that's how we envision Him. The church, British author Dorothy Sayers observed, has pared the claws of the Lion of Judah and made Him like a household pet.[7]

How we got so disconnected from the true identity of Jesus found in the Gospels, I will never know. But He is a true example of what it means to be a risk taker. He lived the most hazardous and endangered life one could live, so it makes sense that His followers are to be dangerous and countercultural, too. His desire is that, as His people, we become a spittin' image of Him in how we live and act and dream and eat and work and play.

Jesus learned how to risk from the one who could teach Him: His Dad. God the Father is known as being a daring, dangerous God. That's why He's described in Scripture as a mighty warrior (see Exodus 15:3). Jesus learned the pattern of courage and adventure from His Father. Mike Yaconelli, in his book *Dangerous Wonder*, wrote, "Our world is populated with domesticated grownups who would rather settle for safe, predictable answers instead of wild, unpredictable mystery. Faith has been reduced to a comfortable set of *beliefs* about God instead of an *un*comfortable encounter *with* God."[8] The God of the Bible is our true example for living life to the fullest, and that means being uncomfortable and unsafe.

21

It may be a disappointing reality to some of us that in order to follow Jesus, we can't remain safe and secure. Actually, living safely is in diametric opposition to following Christ. Nowhere in Scripture are we promised that real life won't have a costly price tag. In fact, if this life is as true and valuable as Jesus says it is, then it can't be cheap and easily attainable. Climbing to the top of a fourteen-thousand-foot mountain is much more rewarding than climbing onto your couch, because it requires much more of us. That's just the way it works.

So, how *do* you define a risk taker? I think, if I'm getting this right, that a risk taker is someone who obeys God even if obedience is difficult or uncomfortable or, um, risky. In this book, you'll read about different people in Scripture who help us define what risk truly is. As you read, you'll find that each chapter focuses on an ordinary person who lived in a culture different from ours but at the same time experienced life and situations similar to ours.

The characters found in Scripture don't exist merely to teach us about biblical history, although knowing history is certainly beneficial. They are not frozen in time to be admired behind museum glass. Their stories are alive and active, significant to us today. They invite us and inspire us to jump into the pages of a Bigger Story, a story that God is continuing to write at this very moment. The ordinary but truly honorable people we'll explore in these pages put a gentle hand on our shoulders and invite us to study their lives so that ours can become richer, fuller, and more like the way God planned.

Yes, I have risked. I hope I am always able to risk everything for the just and right cause.

—Edward Walker, in *The Village*

If there isn't a God nothing matters, but if there is a God nothing else matters.

—H. G. Wells

REBELLING FOR A GOOD CAUSE

SHADRACH, MESHACH, AND ABEDNEGO

n Detroit is a wonderful little tourist attraction called Greenfield Village. I usually hate tourist traps, but this place intrigued me. Henry Ford, the car man himself, developed the quaint little village. Ford was an avid collector of history, and because of his great wealth, he was able to purchase significant artifacts from U.S. history (such as the chair Abraham Lincoln sat in when he was assassinated).[1] Ford didn't purchase just small artifacts; he purchased *entire buildings* from around the country. He unearthed them carefully, loaded them onto a trailer, and transported them to Detroit, where he set them up in his village. On that same street in Greenfield Village, you can see the childhood home of Noah Webster (the dictionary guy), the laboratory of Thomas Edison, and the bicycle shop the Wright Brothers worked at before they flew their first airplane. You'd think that to visit all these places you'd have to travel the country, but they're within six city blocks of one another.

As I toured, I was most fascinated by a large green and yellow bus made famous in racially segregated Montgomery, Alabama. The city bus traveled route 2875 through town. I had chills when I was able to sit in the exact seat where a certain African-American seamstress once sat. Most of us know the story. After a long day at work, she entered the bus, sat in the front, and refused to give up her seat. The bus driver said, "You had better give up your seat to this white gentleman waiting to sit down."

She calmly said, "No, I will not move."

The driver turned around again and said, "Excuse me, if you don't get up from your seat, I will stop this bus, go get a policeman, and have you arrested."

"So be it," she said.

And with those words on a hot summer afternoon in 1955, Rosa Parks birthed the beginning of America's Civil Rights Movement. An ordinary seamstress got on a bus on an ordinary day, on an ordinary route, and took an extraordinary risk. She did get arrested, she probably knew she would, but regardless, she stood for truth—the truth that no person is better than another. Her bravery changed the face of American history. As I sat in her famous seat and listened to the tour guide talk about that fateful day, I wondered what would have happened had Rosa Parks not given up her seat. And I then wondered how I could stand up for truth as she had.

Like a Sore Thumb

When I think about standing up for truth, the first thing that comes to mind is *holiness*. Back in the Old Testament, God said, "Be holy because I, the LORD your God, am holy" (Leviticus 19:2). When we hear the word *holy*, it's easy to think of someone who spouts Bible verses incessantly, attends church every night of the week, and doesn't know how to have fun. But when the word *holy* is used in Scripture, it refers to being different or set apart, not lame.

God is holy, the Most Holy, because He is set apart from all of us. We are sinful, selfish people; He is blameless. We are weak; He is all-powerful and all-knowing. There is nothing in the entire universe that could compare to God; therefore, He is different, unique, and set apart from everything else. (That's probably why He's so popular.) So when God says we are to be holy, He is calling us, His people, to be unique and different and set apart from all other people. Being holy often means standing out in a crowd. Long ago, God created laws and rules (including those weird laws that make us scratch our heads)[2] as a way for His people to be set apart. He didn't do this to control His people and keep them from having fun; He did this so they would live fulfilling lives, distinct from the neighboring countries, so the neighboring countries would know above all else that it was God behind all this holiness and He would then get the credit.

But we don't find this "setting apart" in just the Old Testament. The books of Acts and Romans and most of the letters written by Paul to the churches are actually records of people who lived differently from the rest of the culture. In the first century, the Roman Empire was ruling much of the known world, including Israel. Caesar's power and rule was far-reaching. There were laws in the Roman Empire stating that everyone must acknowledge that Caesar was Lord. If you refused to make such a claim, you could be killed.

But during that time, Jesus stormed into the story by claiming that Caesar was not Lord, *He* was. And Jesus' controversial message generated groups of believers all over the place. These people were, of course, called Christians. Because of their message, they faced ridicule, torture, and death. But regardless, they maintained their stance because they knew the truth and believed it was the only thing worth standing for.

The Roman government tried to kill these Christians, but the more they tried, the more the Christian movement gained momentum. In fact, the movement spread like wildfire. Their stand for the truth that Jesus was Lord raised them to levels of unimaginable influence, as recorded in the book of Acts.[3]

Paul wrote to many of these followers of Jesus who lived in Rome and were being persecuted for their refusal to acknowledge that Caesar was Lord. He wrote that when Christians live as passionate followers of Jesus, the world begins to look and say, "There's something different about you—but in a good and intriguing way. What is it?" Paul knew to remind us that being different is good. He sensed a magnetic pull for Christians to conform to the ways in which the world operates. And it's no different today than it was in the first century, when Paul wrote, "Do not conform any longer to the pattern of this world, but be transformed by the renewing of your mind" (Romans 12:2). Blending in is exactly the opposite of what God wants. He desires for us to stand out—just as He does, just as Jesus did—and only then will we attract people to Him, because only then will we help people see His holiness.

About six months ago, I was involved in a spiritual conversation with a guy in his mid-twenties who was far from God. As I was talking about what it means to be a follower of Jesus, he interrupted me and asked, "Why would I want to be a Christian when the Christians I know live exactly the same kind of life that I live? What difference would being a Christian make in my life?"

People everywhere—whether or not they acknowledge it like my friend did—are watching those who claim to be different and bold in their convictions. Your level of influence may not be a job promotion doubling your salary, it may not be a lucrative autobiography that lands on the *New York Times* best-seller list, but it will surely grow as people say, "I don't always agree with what you do, but I admire your courage to stand up for what is right."

Rebels with a Cause

If you grew up in the church, you probably learned the following story in Sunday school while making a craft or eating graham crackers. The story is recorded in the third chapter of Daniel, and it's about three teenage men named Shadrach, Meshach, and Abednego.[4] If you received your pin for good attendance in Sunday school, you're probably thinking that you know this story so well, you could write a chapter on it with your eyes closed. But I'm going to ask you, and help you, to shed the shell of familiarity and begin to look at this story—a story about holiness and risk and influence—with a fresh outlook. (If you're *not* familiar with this story, I sense you might be at a greater advantage because it is so easy for most of us to put our minds on autopilot.)

Here's a little background. The Jews, God's chosen people, were overthrown by a group of foreigners from the north, the Babylonians.[5] Captured and dragged away by a cruel and powerful king named Nebuchadnezzar, the Jews found themselves surrounded by new gods, customs, and languages. As if that wasn't enough, three Jews in particular—Shadrach, Meshach, and Abednego (who happened to be friends with Daniel, by the way)—were put in leadership right under this cruel King Nebuchadnezzar. We don't know for sure why the king had these guys in such an important position of authority, but they must have been pretty sharp, trustworthy, and responsible dudes to have positions of this type of authority in a foreign land. The king tried his best to turn them into the perfect Babylonian boys, but, as Jews, followers of the one true God, they refused to change their unique identity.

Part of maintaining their identity as Jews meant they could not practice certain Babylonian rituals, such as eating certain foods and marrying foreign women and bowing to any god other than Yahweh. God had commanded Israel to be different from every other nation

29

on earth—part of the holiness issue—and blending in would have been disobedience to God.

So, the story goes that one day, King Nebuchadnezzar (who, by the way, some say paralleled the behaviors of Saddam Hussein) built an image of gold ninety feet high and nine feet wide, which most scholars believe was built to honor the pagan god Nebo. Nebo was the God of wisdom in Babylonian religion, and King Nebuchadnezzar's name is derived from this deity.[6] In order to show reverence for and submission to these pagan gods, the king would require his subjects to bow in a prostrate position.[7] Subjects would put their knees and foreheads on the ground at this ceremony, similar to how Muslim worshipers bow and pray five times a day.

On one particular day in Babylon, the music played and every forehead touched the ground, except for those of three young men. There they stood, amongst thousands of bowing people, feeling taller than they'd ever felt before. Can you imagine how vulnerable and awkward they felt? And as if feeling tall and awkward wasn't bad enough, these guys knew their fate: If they didn't bow, they would sizzle in the infamous fiery furnace. It was known throughout the land that there would be great consequences for rebellion against the king.

When the king found out about their refusal to bow, he said, "Is it true, Shadrach, Meshach, and Abednego, that you don't respect my gods and refuse to worship the gold statue that I have set up? I'm giving you a second chance—but from now on, when the big band strikes up you must go to your knees and worship the statue I have made. If you don't worship it, you will be pitched into a roaring furnace, no questions asked. Who is the god who can rescue you from my power?" (Daniel 3:14-15, MSG). The boys confirmed that yes, it's true, they won't bow, and yes, it's true, they trust their God. And for some reason, but we're not told why, the king gives them a second chance.

In the king's merciful response, however, his sarcasm is clear. It's as if he says, "I don't know if you had some wax buildup in your ears and you couldn't hear the music, and I don't know if you saw everyone else bowing on the ground, but you better get up off your butts and down on your knees, fellas, before you get smoked." Most of us, if confronted with this situation, would look at our buddies and then back at the king and say, "Hold on. We had no idea that not bowing would make you so mad. Whatever you say, sir. We're happy to bow." But we all know that Shadrach, Meshach, and Abednego didn't recant, apologize, ask for another chance, or plead temporary insanity. In front of the most powerful person in the Middle East, they didn't back down. They were surely afraid, but the truth they stood for motivated them more than impending death.

What's so great about Shadrach, Meshach, and Abednego's story is that our opportunities in life are no different. The story, if we really think about it, forces us to look in the face of the choices we have before us. In verses 16-17, the guys' words cement their choice to obey God over the king: "O Nebuchadnezzar, we do not need to defend ourselves before you in this matter. If we are thrown into the blazing furnace, the God we serve is able to save us from it, and he will rescue us from your hand, O king" (MSG).

31

They understood that truth, God's truth, is bigger than whatever consequences they may face. And although they were willing to burn in the fiery furnace for the sake of obeying their God (see verse 18), we know that the Lord saved them anyway by sending His angel into the fire to protect them.

Everyday Life or Life-Threatening

Shadrach, Meshach, and Abednego's story reminds me of the final scene in *Braveheart*. (Yes, it's true, I like *Braveheart* a lot. I'm a guy—what can I say?)

William Wallace is being tried for the charge of treason against the king. The king brings him in front of the entire village, and he whispers to him during the torture, "You will fall on your knees now, declare yourself the king's loyal subject, and beg his mercy and you shall have it." Given the opportunity to bow, Wallace refuses to do so as he writhes in pain. He stands up for what is right even though the cost is extremely high.

If you have watched this scene in the movie, you know there is something very meaningful, very magnetic, that draws us in. It stirs us and touches at the very core of our emotions. Why? Because we've been in situations (though admittedly less dramatic) in which we've had a decision to make: cave in and go the easy route, or stand up for the convictions we hold to even though the cost is great. And we're forced to ask ourselves, *Did we stand, or did we fold?*

32   So, you may be thinking right now, *Yeah, maybe if I were in a life-threatening situation, I could see the difference between standing for truth and bowing down, but in my everyday life, the line is blurrier.* I agree. Yes, a life-threatening situation makes you think just a bit harder about the decisions you make. But, on the other hand, the Lord *does* implore us to be holy, every day—period—so it's probably good to be aware of whatever this call to holiness means in your life. I honestly think this is a matter of having a consistent conversation with God. What does *He* think about what you are doing or not doing? I bet the Holy Sprit would be quite willing to provide His thoughts. To be in communication with God on a regular basis provides the strength and ability to know what's right and stand for it.

It is not easy to stand out, in any culture, because people conform to one another naturally. (You know, like when you spend a lot of time with someone, you start to sound alike, act alike, look alike . . .) Most Americans, for example, eat at the same restaurants (mostly), shop at the same stores (again, mostly), and drive the same cars because those are just standard ways of living in the U.S. God is fully aware of this reality and doesn't expect us to be countercultural for the sake of being countercultural. Again, His purpose is holiness, so there are times when He makes it clear where to draw the line between standing out and blending in.

For me, a time came when I felt convicted about the music I listened to (many of you have probably had a similar experience). So, one summer night when I was in high school, my brother and I went through a fiery-furnace experience of our own. The only difference was, we did have several hairs singed. We gathered up all our CDs that we felt compromised our Christian beliefs, snuck out of the house, and stopped in the middle of our cul-de-sac. Then we sat down cross-legged across from one another, put the CDs in a heaping pile of plasticness, and lit them on fire.

Our ceremonial burning party proved more difficult than we expected. While paper burns quickly, we realized the glossy lyric jackets and plastic jewel cases do not. My brother and I had to hold down a lighter on the lyric jackets for minutes on end before they would ignite. As we tirelessly attempted to burn these practically non-flammable items, we talked about how much money we had spent on them, how much we enjoyed the music, and how it was all going to end up as ash. But we knew getting rid of the CDs was necessary because we were reminded of God's call to holiness and we knew the music was getting in the way.

During our conversation, a spark flew off the pile and hit a lighter right by my knee. The lighter ignited immediately, like a flash of lightning, into a gigantic ball of flames, engulfing everything. It happened in a split second.[8] Although we were scared stiff, we were unharmed. The huge explosion didn't affect my brother, but

33

it had seared off my eyelashes, eyebrows, and all the hair on my shins and forearms.

We quickly realized that our bonfire was probably not the best way to get the job done—okay, it definitely wasn't the best way—but we felt good about our decision and thanked God we were still alive. Before we retreated back inside the house, we prayed Mom and Dad wouldn't find out (a self-indulgent prayer, to be sure). I took a lengthy shower and washed several times so my mother would not detect the odor of burnt hair.[9]

My brother and I have reminisced about that story, and we've talked about it in the context of Shadrach, Meshach, and Abednego. From our own meager furnace experience to the unimaginable heat in the guys' furnace experience, we praise God for His grand miracle and know the difficulty of being holy is nothing compared to the reward. Eugene Peterson writes:

> Obedience to God in the pressures and stresses of day-by-day living and trust in God's ways in the large sweep of history are always at risk. . . . Obedience to God is difficult when we are bullied into compliance to the God-ignoring culture out of sheer survival. Trust in God is likewise at risk of being abandoned in favor of the glamorous seductions of might and size. . . .
>
> There was little or no observable evidence in the circumstances to commend against-the-stream obedience or overarching trust. . . .
>
> Very few of us live in settings congenial to God-loyalty and among people who affirm a costly discipleship. Hardly a day goes by that we do not have to choose between compliance to what is expedient and loyalty to our Lord.[10]

The story of Shadrach, Meshach, and Abednego is not some distant, backwoods story we read like a child's fairy tale that gives us a warm-fuzzy feeling before we go to sleep. We have to understand that we are part of this story *now*. You and I are called to live lives that are different from those in the world around us because then we will be a true influence in the name of Christ. By definition, risk will cost us something of value. You're not really risking if you aren't sacrificing something valuable to you, even if that something is the feeling of comfort, acceptance, or being safe. But the joy in all this sacrifice is that God promises a holy life to be not only fulfilling but also glorifying to God. And that is the best sort of life we could live.

Here's an example. One day back in 1975, a freshman named Dave heard his biology professor claim that evolution without God was the explainable truth for how the world came to be. Dave felt called to express the untruth of the professor's statement. He stood up in the middle of class and politely but boldly refuted his professor's claim, stating that as a follower of Jesus, he could not accept his professor's claim because he knew that God was indeed responsible for creating the universe. After class was over, a brunette named Debbie approached Dave and told him she appreciated his courage to stand up for what was right.

And that was the first time my mom and dad met.

That's just one example of how God turns what can seem to be the most simple, insignificant experiences into stories of great worth and influence. Without my dad's stand for truth, I probably would not be here writing this book. Without Rosa Park's front-seat stand, our nation could quite possibly still be segregated. Without Shadrach, Meshach, and Abednego, the eyes of King Nebudachnezzar might never have opened to see a God he had never taken seriously. For the first time, the king was able to see just how powerful this God was

35

that Shadrach and Company claimed to believe. We never would have had this story in our Bibles, nor the opportunity to learn from the example of three guys who stood up for what they believed, and God was honored in the process. Who knows what God can do—and how He will influence the world, the future, and His kingdom—if we choose to obey His call to holy different-ness.

Going Further

1. Why is it so difficult to be different from everyone else? As Christians, why is it important?

2. Read Romans 12:1-2. What does it mean for us to live our lives in such a way? How does this verse help us influence our world for Jesus?

3. What are the statues in our culture that try to seduce you into bowing?

4. Although the fiery furnace might be a familiar passage to you, what new insights do you now have about this story?

5. Shadrach, Meshach, and Abednego stood for truth in a life-threatening situation, but what does it look like for you to stand for truth on, say, an ordinary Tuesday afternoon?

Two roads diverged in a wood, and I took the one less traveled by, and that has made all the difference.

— Robert Frost

You think God is going to come into your . . . house, look around, and see that you just need a new floor or better furniture and that everything needs just a little cleaning . . . then you look out the window one day and see that there's a wrecking ball outside. It turns out that God actually thinks your whole foundation is shot and you're going to have to start from scratch.

— Marianne Williamson

DUMPING $50K ON A PAIR OF 2 DIRTY FEET

MARY, THE SISTER OF LAZARUS

ou and Cathy, good friends of mine, recently made a decision that would leave most friends and family members scratching their heads. Lou had worked in a well-paying six-figure finance job. But one day, after many years in this career, he decided to resign from his position and enroll full-time in seminary. With excitement in his voice and some anxiety in his eyes, Lou told the captive audience in his living room, "We're going for it."

This was no midlife crisis for Lou; it was scary, for certain. Together as a family they had decided Cathy would go back to work while Lou studied and went to class. Nowadays, Lou reads textbooks, crams for midterms, and writes papers alongside his daughter, who's in high school. Recently he told me, with a humble smile, that it had been a few years since he last listened to lectures, took notes, and studied for midterms. He doesn't have specific plans for his seminary degree, but he's certain the rigorous biblical training will never be wasted, whether he decides to enter into full-time vocational ministry or not.

I am sure Lou and Cathy have gotten their fair share of interesting responses from well-meaning friends and family ("Are you *sure* this is the right decision?"). When they made this decision, they were well aware of the consequences: a huge financial setback, complete rearrangement of schedules, total lifestyle change. But for my friends, this decision was about serving God in the best way they could and in the way they felt He desired of them. They wanted to join God on the adventure He'd laid out for them, individually and as a family, which meant arranging their priorities to meet His. The world and its drive for power and success and financial gain would think they're nuts, but I think they've got courage.

This idea of risking our priorities in order to focus on God and His priorities is found all over the place in Scripture (such as the first commandment, "You should have no other gods before me" [Exodus 20:3]). But there's one particular woman in the New Testament who I think demonstrates this kind of undistracted attention to God better than most.

42

In the Gospels, we find a story about Jesus having dinner with friends in a town called Bethany. Bethany, on the back side of the Mount of Olives, is about a mile's walk east from the temple in Jerusalem. John chapter 12 records that Jesus had close friends who lived in this small village, including Lazarus (whom He raised from the dead),[1] Mary (Lazarus's sister), and Martha (also his sister). Similar gospel accounts tell us that this particular dinner party included guests such as Lazarus, Martha, Mary, Judas Iscariot, and probably Jesus' other eleven disciples. In Jesus' time, sharing meals carried incredible significance. It didn't mean just grabbing a burger and fries with some buddies. To share a meal in Jewish culture was to communicate that you loved and trusted and accepted those with whom you were dining.[2] Matthew's gospel records that this dinner was in honor of Jesus and hosted by a leper named Simon (see Matthew 26:6).

I don't know if you know much about the horrific skin disease called leprosy, but to say that Simon was an eyesore would have been a gross understatement. It's hard to grasp the violence of this disease because although it was a big problem in the first century, the progress of science and medicine has almost eliminated leprosy from North America and most of the world. It's a devastating disease. It destroys the nerves in the body, making one unable to feel pain or heat or pressure and causing skin to turn white as a sheet. Because those with leprosy are unable to feel pain, they live life literally numb. There have been reports of lepers accidentally searing their hand on a hot stovetop without even knowing it.[3]

On a mission trip to India, I actually encountered someone with leprosy. During a break between activities, a few of us decided to hike up a mountain that overlooked the city. The trail to the top cut through the center of a very small village. The local people were amazed that westerners would come to their village. Though we were clueless as to what they were saying, we were sure that on every street corner, we were the topic of conversation. As I stopped to smile, wave, and snap a few pictures, I felt a light tug on my pant leg. I looked down and saw a middle-aged woman (well, at least I *think* she was a woman — it was hard to tell) sitting cross-legged on the ground looking up at me.

43

Her face was more distorted and disfigured than any I had ever seen. She looked like a character out of a horror movie that really freaks you out and gives you nightmares for a week. She had no teeth, no nose. Flies circled the open sores on her cheeks. Her wounds were evidence of her accidental self-mutilation from not being able to feel pain. Although the woman was Indian, her skin was white as a sheet. Her feet looked like chopped-down tree stumps, and her fingerless hands could have passed for salad tongs.

I jumped back, shocked by the sight, yet she kept looking and asking for help in a language I could not understand. I was also fearful and ignorant, unaware if leprosy was contagious and if I was now running the risk of contracting this awful disease. It turns out that leprosy is not contagious.

Since this experience, I've often wondered if Simon looked at all like this woman from India. How disfigured was his body? How badly was his face gnarled and misshapen? At dinnertime, if Jesus asked him to pass the bread, would he have been able to accomplish this simple task? Did he need help going to the bathroom? Did he frighten children as he hobbled along to the market?

Simon probably lived in Bethany because he wasn't allowed to live in Jerusalem. Considered unclean, lepers were not allowed to live inside the city and were restricted to certain areas outside of town limits. Maybe Simon settled in Bethany because it was one of the few locations on the outskirts of town that would allow him to take up residence. In fact, to associate with lepers was not seen as a social faux pas; it was unimaginable. Even the worst Jew would never interact with a leper. It would make one ceremonially unclean and would require one to live outside the city for a period of time. Mary would have been taking a large risk just to be around and in close quarters at the home of a man with leprosy.

Sweet-Smelling Feet

During social hour at Simon's house, Mary entered with an alabaster jar of very expensive perfume made of pure nard.[4] This perfume was extracted from a tree root imported from India. In the first century, owning a bottle of pure nard was a great treasure to be displayed prominently in one's home to impress the neighbors and keep up with the proverbial first-century Joneses. A jar like this would be sealed in a bottle with a long neck. When a time special enough to warrant its use arrived, the bottle would be broken and it would contain just enough ointment for a single use, about an ounce.

Carrying the jar, Mary approached Jesus. She bent to her knees, broke the bottle, and poured the perfume on His feet. Interestingly, her bottle contained a *pint* of pure nard, about twelve ounces.[5] John records that the fragrance of her perfume filled the entire house (see John 12:3).

I know that people today put perfume on their wrists, neck, and arms, among other places, but usually not on their feet. I've never walked into the cosmetics section of a department store and seen a woman slip off her shoes and spray a few squirts on her bunion-covered toes. But in the first century, pouring perfume on the feet of another was a sign of devotion and respect.

In addition, it was not customary for women to let their hair down in the presence of men, especially religious men. When the disciples saw Mary's hair, they might have blushed or looked at the ground, prompted by the embarrassment of the situation. But going a step further, the text says that Mary wiped Jesus' dusty, dirty, cracked feet with her hair. Completely socially unacceptable. But Mary—and Jesus—didn't care. She not only didn't care about the social rules she was breaking by being in the presence of a leper but also had done something that could have been perceived as risqué, perhaps even indecent, in that culture.

I admit, if I saw a woman push her Lexus SUV into a lake, claiming that doing so was a symbol of honor to some nice—even famous—guy, I would probably be shocked and disgusted. So it's understandable that some of the dinner guests who viewed this perfume spectacle were flustered. Judas Iscariot, the man who would betray Jesus, said in great hypocrisy, "Why this waste of perfume? It could have been sold for more than a year's wages and the money given to the poor." A recent report stated that the average American income is just over $50,000.[6] So, in our terms, a jar of perfume broken for Jesus would be worth approximately $50K. We don't know exactly how or why Mary received such a valuable possession. Maybe it was passed down through the generations in her family. There is no way to know for sure, but it certainly was a prized possession — so much so that others also might have speculated about where she would have gotten such as thing.

Because of her "foolishness," she was rebuked harshly by some of the people at the dinner.[7] We don't know exactly who all of these scoffers were — they could have been Simon the Leper or prostitutes or tradesmen from the market or all of Jesus' disciples. We only know that Judas and some other guests were not happy about it.

Risk and Scorn

What does Mary's story have to do with risking our priorities? Lots more than you'd initially think. It's easy to read this story and assume, *That woman must have cared about Jesus a lot to touch His feet.* But what we miss, if we are not careful, is that this woman didn't just touch someone's nasty feet or even waste a lot of money, as Judas accused her of doing. She decided that other priorities in her life—paying her bills, impressing the neighbors, even giving to the poor—came second to her narrow focus on Jesus. She knew somehow that her worship to Jesus was the most important thing she could do with her money, time, and body. I cannot imagine how hard that would be to forfeit my greatest assets, literally, for the sake of worshiping Christ. Talk about a sacrifice of praise. I mean, I often feel my greatest sacrifice of praise is allowing my legs to become sore after a long set of worship songs in church. But the reality is, if we really placed Christ at the center of our lives, we would place parts, if not all, of almost every area in our life on the altar of obedience. There is a subtle but extremely important message here when it comes to our priorities: If God sits in the primary spot of our life, everything else is secondary, at best.

I find it ironic that it was one of the "religious people" around the table that made such an objection. Judas sounded righteous, but in fact he was merely dishonest and greedy. Important rabbis and teachers in the first century would often leave the finances to a trustworthy disciple. Judas spoke up because he was the chairman of the stewardship committee—and, sadly, because he also wanted his cut (see John 12:6). It makes me wonder about the times I have criticized individuals for making a big sacrifice that didn't seem practical or beneficial for what I believed was "the greater good." I'm sure I've done this more than a few times, sometimes without even realizing it. If I haven't verbalized it, I've definitely thought it.

As we well know, Jesus doesn't often respond how we expect Him to. With Mary, He was pleased. With the scoffers, He was annoyed: "Lay off. Leave her alone. Mind your own business. She's doing the right thing." But would giving the money to the poor be bad stewardship? Absolutely not. In fact, giving to the poor is an important priority and one close to the heart of God. Jesus spoke often about giving to the poor. The Old and New Testaments are filled with references to God's heart being with the poor and the downtrodden and how we have a responsibility to help and care for the poor. But the heart of this issue is not about dollars and cents and investments and generosity. What God wants from us is our attention, our focus. And whatever it takes for us to give our heart to Him is what He'll ask for. Our other priorities will then flow from our main priority.

The Center

As I sit here in a quiet coffee shop, I ponder when I last sacrificed a year of *anything*—big or small—to show God my devotion to Him.

I guess that's sort of the point of the season of Lent—sacrificing food or activities or other things we love in order to remind us that Christ is our primary focus in life. I wonder if eliminating distractions reminds us that it is Jesus who desires to be at the forefront of our lives (and it should be our desire to place Him there, too).

If you truly felt that God was calling you to sacrifice a year—or more—of something significant to you in worship, what would that something be? Why would sacrificing it be hard for you? I usually find that if I am willing to wrestle with why something is so difficult, I can usually get to the bottom of the issue, and at the bottom, I usually find I've poorly arranged my priorities.

In his book *Under the Overpass*, student Mike Yankoski writes of his education at a reputable Christian college. At this college, he spent every day learning about and thinking about God. But, he says, he soon realized that while he devoted a lot of time to getting to know about God, he had never been forced—or forced himself—to sacrifice something so huge that he could *rely only on* God. He wrote, "I claimed that Christ was my stronghold, my peace, my sustenance, my joy. But I did all that from the safety of my comfortable upper-middle-class life. I never really had to put my claims to the test."[8]

One day in church he had an idea. He thought, *What if I stepped out of my comfortable life with nothing but God and put my faith to the test alongside those who live with nothing every day?*[9] So Mike, along with his friend Sam, decided to become homeless. Leaving behind money, security, health, certainty, and almost everything but a backpack and sleeping bag, they lived for five months in several cities sleeping under bridges, in parks, and in shelters, and eating meals from trash cans and soup kitchens. No phones, no credit card or cash, no extra clothing.[10] Just them and God. They did all this to experience what it meant to make God their number one priority. Though they had nothing else, they had Him, and that was all that mattered.

Mike and Sam symbolically broke a perfume bottle by volunteering to participate in this adventure. Mike wrote that a lesson he learned during his homelessness was "the comfort and security we strive so hard to create for ourselves doesn't even come close to the 'life in the full' that Christ promises."[11] Only when we trade our self-made priorities for a life fully focused on Christ will we know what it really means to follow Him.

Good Versus the Best

It's not like all our priorities are bad, though. Staying healthy and loving our neighbor are priorities God commands of us, but what's interesting is that sometimes even good priorities can be the biggest enemy to the most important priorities. Jim Collins, in his book *Good to Great*, writes in the book's first sentence, "Good is the enemy of great."[12] As a pastor, sometimes I get involved in projects that, from the outside, seem like good projects to be committed to, and they probably *are* good. But they can ultimately be detrimental because they keep me from the priorities that are the most important—the areas that deserve my full attention, focus, and concern. It's strange to think that even the good things can keep us from placing Christ at the center of our lives. When this happens, I've learned, those good things are no longer good. I think this is why at the beginning of his letter to the church in Philippi, Paul prayed that "your love may abound more and more in knowledge and depth of insight, so that you may be able to discern *what is best*" (Philippians 1:9-10, emphasis added). God makes it clear He wants us to discern not what is good but what is best—and then do it wholeheartedly. It's easy to do the good thing, but for the most part, it is extremely difficult to choose to do the *best* thing.

49

"Only One Thing Is Needed"

In chapter 10 of Luke, we find another story involving the same Mary. Jesus accepts an invitation for dinner at Lazarus, Mary, and Martha's home.[13] We all know how this story goes: Martha is frantic over dinner preparations (a task that is necessary to getting dinner done) while Mary, once again, focuses all her attention on Jesus, being completely useless to Martha. Martha gets jealous and frustrated, which leads her to complain to Jesus. To which Jesus replies, "Only one thing is needed. Mary has chosen what is better, and it will not be taken away from her" (Luke 10:42). It's a lesson about priorities. Mary chose the *best* way.

This can be quite a frustrating story for us because, hey, the food needed to be cooked. They needed to eat. So just because Mary was irresponsible doesn't mean Martha should get the rebuke for getting the job done. Here's what I think: It says in the Bible that God doesn't see what we humans see; He sees the heart (see 1 Samuel 16:7). Maybe in both of Mary's stories, what needed work was the scoffers and complainers, not Mary. I mean, who knows, maybe the food was already cooked and Martha was frantic over finding perfect napkin holders or candle sconces to impress the guests. Maybe Martha and the dinner guests had their priorities set on something other than God's glory, so Jesus demonstrated where the *best* priorities come from: full attention to Him.

As the World Turns

I remember learning about the solar system in Ms. Cleveland's fourth-grade class. We were assigned a research project about the planets—a handwritten page for each one, a sizable project in fourth grade—and then we were to build a model to bring in to class. I constructed the model with the help of my dad by painting an old box dark blue and connecting the planets with fishing line.

50

I was fascinated by the fact that everything revolved around the sun. From that point on, I looked at Virginia sunsets differently than I had before. It was later in ninth-grade history that I learned of Nicolaus Copernicus, who in the medieval period reported his theory that the sun did not revolve around the earth, as popular belief held, but instead the earth around the sun. This went against all of the religious and philosophical beliefs of his time. Galileo then embraced these Copernican ideas some fifty years later and was eventually sentenced to life in prison for his beliefs. Copernicus (and Galileo) were scorned for their "stupidity."[14]

Later, of course, they would be known as the fathers of modern astronomy. Talk about a lesson in priorities. Our modern-day beliefs tell us that everything revolves around me. Eat, drink, and be merry, right? Then we find Jesus, through whom God makes clear the world revolves around the Son (I know, it's cheesy, but it's profoundly true).

Often, as followers of Jesus, our "screwed-up" priorities, as the world would call them, make us a laughingstock. But when we truly engage in the ongoing process of sacrificing the Priority of Me and replacing it with Christ as the center, God does the spiritual transformation—the work of reprogramming the wires of our hearts to be connected to a different and divine source of energy. We know this sacrifice is risky because it places everything intentionally and deliberately in the backseat. We could lose what's most important to us, whether that's money or a relationship or future plans or drugs or whatever.

What are your jars that need breaking? What are the priorities that need to be brought to the feet of Jesus and smashed as a way to communicate to Him that He is most important to you? Right now you're probably in a transitional time in your life, whether you're in

51

high school, soon to enter college, or in college and soon to enter the world beyond. The best time to center your priorities is now. You have many decisions coming up, lots of plans to make, lots of life lessons to be learned. What better way to face those decisions and plans and lessons than with a heart focused on Christ?

There are possessions and positions and people and kings of all kinds who fight daily for the exclusive spot on the throne of your heart, but there is room for only one King on that throne. There are lots of kings that could be labeled *good*, but nothing is more important than placing Jesus — the *best* thing — as number one in your life.

Going Further

1. When we put Christ at the center of our lives, what might need to be sacrificed?

2. What role does security play in your relationship with God and the priorities you choose?

3. Comfort and security aren't always bad things in our relationship with Christ. How can we decide whether comfort and security are helping or hurting our relationship?

4. Can you think of any "good" areas of your life that stand in the place of what's "best"?

5. What are the specific ways you must sacrifice "the Priority of Me"?

Avoiding danger is no safer in the long run than outright exposure. Life is either a daring adventure, or nothing.

—Helen Keller

Do you think I speak this strong in order to manipulate crowds? Or curry favor with God? Or get popular applause? If my goal was popularity, I wouldn't bother being Christ's slave.

—the apostle Paul

RUINING YOUR
3 REPUTATION

Whenever we tell the Christmas story, we usually focus on the character of Mary. She did, after all, play a pretty significant role in giving birth to God-in-the-flesh in a small town outside of Jerusalem. But most times when we tell or read the Christmas story, we whiz right past another important character: Joseph, the earthly father of Jesus. Don't get me wrong: Mary and Jesus are important (that's an understatement), but there is much that Joseph can teach us, too. In fact, the more I contemplate the life of Joseph, the more impressed I am with the guy. He's definitely one of the unsung heroes of our faith.

I wish I lived like Joseph. He was an ordinary dude, as ordinary as one could be. He was undistinguished and unexceptional by all the standards of his day. He was a carpenter in a little town tucked far away from anything that would ever hit the front cover of the *Galilee Post*, but God used this young guy to help change the trajectory of human history.

Marriage Without Benefits

Matthew chapter one tells us that Mary and Joseph were betrothed. Scholars tell us Joseph was probably in his twenties or early thirties and Mary was a young teenager.[1] When a girl experienced her first period, her parents would begin to talk with other parents about arranging a marriage. Betrothal in the first century was much different from engagement in our culture. It wasn't just about giddily showing off the rock on your hand, purchasing bridal magazines, and picking out the perfect caterer. Being betrothed, which customarily lasted a year, pretty much secured that you *were* married, except that you couldn't have sex — basically, marriage without the benefits. This betrothal was so binding that had Joseph been run over by an ox cart and died, Mary would have been considered a widow.

So it goes that one day during their betrothal, Mary went to Joseph and proclaimed she was pregnant. Can you imagine how that conversation went? "Mary, you're *what?!?!* But we never . . . Explain this one to me. Is this what they're calling it these days: 'inspiration from the Holy Spirit'?" I'm sure Joseph wrestled with this new event through sleepless nights. He probably knew he shouldn't marry someone who was unfaithful, but what could he do?

The text says, "Because Joseph her husband[2] was a righteous man and did not want to expose her to public disgrace, he had in mind to divorce her quietly" (Matthew 1:19).[3] He didn't want to humiliate and embarrass the woman whom he had committed to and loved. We often miss the significance of this detail. Old Testament Jewish law stated that Mary, even in a betrothal, could have been stoned for this offense. In fact, Joseph, by all standards of the day, *should* have had Mary stoned.[4] If he wouldn't, people would then look down on *him*. Any righteous Jew, by first-century standards, would have made a spectacle of Mary, divorcing her loudly and obnoxiously, publicly exposing her to the embarrassment of her future as an adulteress and unwed mother, and plastering her picture with some incriminating headline in the morning papers. Joseph's refusal to do any of this was unacceptable according to the religious and cultural standards of his day, but to God, "he was a righteous man."

Listening to Dreams

As Joseph considered his options for handling the situation, God appeared to him in a dream. Somehow, until recently, I'd glanced over the fact that Joseph didn't have just *one* dream in this story but *four* dreams that carried a great amount of significance. My dream last night involved breaking up a gunfight in a department store and being the hero the next day in the newspaper. Not exactly earth-shattering.

Joseph was surely ridiculed to no end by many religious leaders of that day as well as his neighbors. Certainly, those around him judged him for his seemingly foolish decision. Can you imagine the reaction of Joseph's friends as he walked through town? "Joseph, you believe that stuff? You really believe what Mary says is true?" (It's not like Joseph could hide the fact that his fiancée was pregnant. Can you imagine how difficult it might have been for Mary to even walk to the market to buy food, or how her pregnancy might have damaged business for Joseph?

But as Joseph obeyed God through each of the four dreams (after God asked Joseph to stay with Mary, He then told him to move to Egypt because the evil King Herod was trying to kill Jesus, then to move back home once Herod was dead, and then to move again to a small town called Nazareth), he demonstrated that his true calling—to be Jesus' father, the earthly father of the Son of God—was a much more significant calling than the desire to protect his ego. Can you imagine if Joseph *had* chosen to protect his reputation? He would have obeyed the religious leaders' laws and, therefore, had a pregnant Mary stoned, killing her and her unborn, holy child.

Religious Leaders and Flossing

Contrary to Joseph, who acted in obedience to God, many religious leaders of that day operated out of a deep-seated fear of others' opinions. They were afraid people would stop trusting their leadership. They were afraid that other religious leaders would reject them. They were afraid of God. They were afraid of being exposed.[5]

I confess, at times I am like those religious leaders. I fear being found out. I fear that somehow people will reject me because they've decided I'm not qualified to be a pastor (I haven't even completed seminary), I'm not very experienced (I've been a pastor for about three years), and I often don't know what the heck I'm doing when I preach or officiate weddings or do pastoral counseling or write a book. And these fears drive much of my behavior, much of the time. It's kind of like going to the dentist. I rarely floss (about twice a year), but I don't want the dentist to chastise me about not flossing, so I floss the morning before my appointment, thinking that maybe he'll be fooled. Maybe the dental hygienist will lean over and say, "Wow, your teeth look really good. Looks like you've been flossing."

As a pastor, I often try to hide the things that I fear could hurt my reputation. I avoid mentioning my lack of credentials and work extra hard at sounding experienced. The truth, though, is that people who know these things about me respect and love me and trust me just the same as those who don't because they know that God put me here and is working through me. If only I would focus on God's role in this more than my own.

I think focus on God was the major edge Joseph had over the religious leaders. Of course he had a reputation to uphold and could have done so by frantically trying to keep skeletons hidden in his closet, like the fact that his wife was impregnated by a spirit. But Joseph chose to focus on God's words to him in the dreams; he knew he was participating in God's bigger story and that the story was not about him and his life and his reputation. What an incredible role model he must have been to Jesus as His earthly father.

We all can learn a thing or two from Joseph. I'm sure most of us would admit that we, in some way, fear being found out. We fear that someone will learn something about us that is unflattering or unholy. And I'm not suggesting that we spill all our sin beans or announce our inadequacies to everyone we meet, but I do believe that if we stop caring so much about our own personal glory (looking good or perfect or like we have it all together), we could then focus on the enhancement of God's glory. Our reputations pale in comparison to the greater story of God, and if we choose to hold tightly to our own image, it's likely our influence in this world will be significantly limited.

Ironically, the times I realize I am living not for myself but for something — Someone — greater and more powerful than I am are when I actually feel a greater sense of adequacy and worth. To think that by risking my own personal reputation I could truly influence, for Christ, the lives of the people around me is a serious confidence booster. Conversely, the times when I'm not willing to risk my reputation are usually when I am most aware of the opinions of people around me. During those times, my desire becomes to make everyone around me think I'm cool, like I have everything together. This converse relationship reminds me of Proverbs 29:25, which says, "The fear of human opinion disables; trusting in GOD protects you from that" (MSG). I can get pretty paralyzed by my fear of others, and this paralysis keeps me from being obedient and risking as Joseph did much of the time. Author Leo Horrigan writes, "We buy things we don't need, with money we don't have, to impress friends we don't have time for."[6] Yup,

I do that. We've become so skilled at creating and displaying ornate masks in order to portray what we think people want us to be.

Sox the Fox

I am reminded of this conflict each time I go to the ballpark. I don't go to the ballpark anymore just to enjoy a game on a Saturday afternoon; instead, I go there to work. Though I am a pastor, I have a small job (actually more of a hobby) that I enjoy doing on the side. The Colorado Springs Sky Sox, based in my hometown, is the Triple-A minor league baseball team for the Colorado Rockies. For the past two seasons, I've been the team's mascot, Sox the Fox.[7]

You're probably wondering why I'm telling you this. Here's why: Every time I put on the suit for a gig—whether I'm hugging babies, pinching the umpire's butt, leading the crowd in a cheer, jumping off a trampoline to dunk a basketball, or signing autographs—I'm always amazed what God teaches me about reputation and mask wearing. Putting on a huge fox head and shaking my furry tail makes people think I'm the coolest thing. Smiles, waves, hugs, high fives, getting my picture taken with beautiful women—you name it, I get it. It's great. I am loved by everyone. But, of course, that is not who I *really* am. (Can you imagine how my wife would feel if I ran around hugging beautiful women all the time?)

After signing autographs in the seventh inning, my job for the evening is done and I retire to the locker room for a quick shower. When I walk out from the locker room in my street clothes and into the crowd once again, I am a nobody. I am just an average-looking individual, like everyone else.

I've often thought about what it would be like to wear the mascot suit for a week. Everywhere I'd go, people would be so glad to see me, hug me, and high-five me. I would be noticed at all times. But then I think of how hot and sweaty I get (I sweat like you wouldn't believe in that thing) and how frustrating it would be to drive or sleep or go to the bathroom or eat in that uniform. Even though the feeling of being loved is thrilling, ultimately I am not Sox the Fox. I'm reminded that I don't have to impress anyone or even care about my reputation because whether I am a celebrity or a nobody, Jesus said that our identity is wrapped up in His, which translates to dying to myself and being the person God has called me to be. That's the risk we all take: refraining from putting on the mascot suit and, instead, exposing who we really are.

I think that's why so many of us love people like Brennan Manning and the late Rich Mullins. They're unpretentious and real and just don't seem to care what people think about them and their rela tionship with Jesus. And even if they do care, it's not enough to keep them from being their true selves. That takes serious courage because they open themselves up to mockery, judgment, rejection, you name it. Regardless, they refuse to put on the mask.

In the Christmas story, Mary's faith is certainly inspiring, but there's something about Joseph's unashamed obedience to God—his refusal of the mask—during confusing times that strikes a chord in me. I'm pretty sure he is my hero. I want to be like him when I grow up. He risked his own reputation to live his life for God even if it made him look like a fool. In the end, he helped raise the Salvation of Humanity and obeyed the voice of God. Maybe he wasn't so foolish after all.

Going Further

1. Why is it that we care so much about what other people think about us?

2. Have you ever taken a risk that made everyone think you had completely lost your mind? What was it? Why did they think the way they did?

3. What do you fear people finding out about you?

4. How is letting go of our reputation linked to influencing others?

5. "We buy things we don't need, with money we don't have, to impress friends we don't have time for." Most of us can identify with that quote. Why? What makes us behave the way we do?

We should not ask, "What is wrong with the world?" for that diagnosis has already been given. Rather, we should ask, "What has happened to the salt and light?"

—John R. W. Stott

One man with courage makes a majority.

—Andrew Jackson

INVESTING IN THE MESSY

4

PHILIP AND THE ETHIOPIAN EUNUCH

ometimes I get nauseous when I hear people talk about evangelism. Sometimes I even feel light-headed when I hear myself talk about it. Hopefully, that won't happen now. I'd hate to throw up while I'm writing this. I know evangelism is important to Christians, but for some reason, hearing or thinking about it makes me recall memories of the "you're-going-to-hell" evangelists on street corners spouting speeches laced with hatred and out-of-date methods. And the word *evangelism* also reminds me of well-intentioned but overzealous evangelists who are so obsessed with communicating the gospel that they forget to engage in any sort of conversation. I know about this from experience, actually. I've participated in my fair share of drive-by witnessings.

In high school, on the road to a weeklong mission trip, our youth group stopped to eat at a mall food court. As we entered the mall, my friend Ben and I discussed how we had not been sharing our faith as often as we should, so we made a pact that we wouldn't leave the mall until we had shared our faith with at least one person. Scanning the endless sea of tables in the food court, we spotted two teenage guys who looked about our age — and we pounced.

After we introduced ourselves, the guys reluctantly invited us to sit down. We shared — maybe *lectured* is the better word — the gospel with them with as much passion and gusto as we could muster.

While we were eager to share the gospel, the two guys were not as eager to hear it. After about five minutes, as they nervously looked at each other, one of them said, "Uh, we're Muslims — gotta go," and then they scurried off. Something told me they weren't really followers of Islam, but I give them credit for their clever answer. While our intentions were good and we were proud of our courage at the time, now that I look back on the situation, I think we did more harm than good. They probably walked away thinking we were members of some obscure cult, the kind that sacrificed animals in the backyard, instead of being encouraged to pursue this man named Jesus. But I've been on the receiving end before, too.

Jesus Isn't a Time-Share Pitch

A little over a year after we got married, my wife and I took a vacation to a bustling Colorado town that boasts one of the elite ski resorts in the West. We went during ski season and before the summer rush to capitalize on cheaper lodging and restaurant deals and the lack of noisy tourists. Walking down Main Street one afternoon, a kind gentleman approached us and told us that if we sat through a ninety-minute presentation on purchasing a time-share, we would receive a one-hundred-dollar voucher that could be used for any restaurant in the town.

"No obligation whatsoever," he assured us. "Just go and listen, and the hundred bucks is yours." We couldn't afford a doghouse in that expensive town, let alone a time-share, but we thought that if there was no obligation, we could manage to sit through an hour-and-a-half presentation in exchange for a few fancy dinners out on the town.

When we arrived for the presentation, we met Eddie, a middle-aged man with a perma-smile and wink that put us immediately on the defensive. Something just wasn't right about him. Megan and I knew before we walked in that we absolutely could not afford what Eddie had to offer us, but we sat through his spiel, wanting to keep up our end of the deal. Eddie's job was to try to convince us that we could, in fact, afford what he was offering. And even if we couldn't afford it, he said, it was such a wonderful, unbelievable price that it would be worth it.

Some interesting events soon unfolded. We started with awkward small talk. Every time Eddie asked us a question, he would interrupt us during our answer to tell us his thoughts instead. It became rather apparent that he didn't care a whole lot about what we had to say or even who we were. We wondered why he even bothered asking us questions in the first place. After the small talk, Eddie steered the conversation to his time-share pitch. His dog-and-pony show included charts and glossy brochures of exotic and luxurious places all over the world. He spouted irrelevant statistics about the property. I thought my head was going to explode.

It didn't matter to us that the place was beautiful—we couldn't afford it, plain and simple. We told him we were not interested, but our adamant words did not discourage or deter him one bit. In fact, it only fueled the fire even more and made him more determined to change our minds. The only answer he wanted to hear from us was, "Sign us up," but we never said those words. *Several* times we not so subtly told him that we weren't interested. Each time I gave a reason, and each time he countered with a rebuttal:

"But where else can you get a deal like this?"

"But this is cheaper than any vacation you could ever take—how could you turn this down?"

"Yes, but this deal lasts only until the end of today. You must act quickly!"

After two hours, he was still enjoying the sound of his own voice, and we were miserable. Our experience had evolved from a conversation, to a sermon, to a monologue, and ultimately to a debate. By the end, I was so frustrated that I hoped it would turn into a wrestling match. I could picture it in my mind: beating the stuffing out of this guy and telling him to shut up (in a Christian love kinda way, of course). We were so fed up with what had transpired over the past two hours, fed up with the fact that our time had been wasted, fed up with feeling duped, fed up with being treated poorly. At this point, we were so upset that if Eddie had given us a week at the time-share for free, we *still* wouldn't have taken it.[1]

Finally, we'd had it. With veins bulging out of my neck, I stood up and leaned over Eddie's desk. Pounding my fist onto his desk, I said, "You promised us this would be an hour and a half, and it's been over *two hours* and you're still talking. Listen to us once and for all: WE'RE NOT INTERESTED IN BUYING. End of discussion. We're leaving now." You probably won't believe this, but he kept talking. And with his mouth still moving, Megan and I left the office and fumed the entire two-hour drive home. As promised, we received our hundred bucks, but it was little consolation.

I've thought about this episode many times. Though it was a situation I would never repeat, and I wouldn't wish it on my worst enemy, we did learn a clear and valuable lesson that day: We soon realized that Eddie's behavior was strikingly similar to the behavior of many Christians when we evangelize. People are buyers, Jesus is the product, and we are the salesmen. We want them to enjoy beautiful heaven, and we want the notches on our belt, so we pitch, pitch, pitch, only to make things worse. But the problem with Eddie's approach is that it's excruciatingly annoying but also horribly safe. It involves absolutely no risk. We don't get personally involved; we stay at a distance. I'm pretty sure that kind of evangelism is not what Jesus had in mind.

It seems that most Christians are perfectly willing to tell people about Jesus, but I am beginning to wonder if that's primarily what we are called to do. Aren't we called to love people first? Certainly telling people about Jesus is important and necessary, but have we skipped a step — the step of loving and serving and caring and valuing people as individuals and seeing them with the eyes of Jesus? There are several times in the Gospels when Jesus approached beggars and paralytics and blind men, and the first thing He did was *not* say, "Hey guys, uh, I don't know you and I don't care, really, but I want to tell you about me and how awesome I am" or "Ladies and gentlemen: I am an extremely busy individual, preaching and healing and battling those dang Pharisees, so if you would all line up in a straight line, I will briefly touch you and you will be healed. I don't have time to stick around and talk to all of you because I am off to another speaking engagement, so if you would be so kind as to let me slip away after I have healed you all I would greatly appreciate your consideration." Of course not. Instead, He asked, "What do you want me to do for you?" (Matthew 20:32). His basic mind-set was *How can I help?* Jesus calls us to risk our own selfish desires, use of time, and comfort zones in order to get closer to people. Really close. Invested.

The problem with becoming invested in people's lives, though, is that you'll probably end up loving them. And loving people can get pretty sticky and involved and time-consuming. It's definitely not convenient. That's why it's much easier to go on a mission trip to Uganda for two weeks than it is to serve in your own hometown or neighborhood. By going to Uganda, you can tell people about Jesus during the week and then leave and never see them again. You drive by, shoot them with words, but starve them of love.

Philip and the Man with No Genitals

I am not an expert when it comes to sharing my faith, and I don't know too many people who are, so I take great encouragement from a New Testament risk taker by the name of Philip, who proved to be a great example in the evangelism category. Philip let availability and a willingness to invest direct him, and then he let spiritual conversation follow.

Acts chapter 8 gives the details surrounding the story of Philip's obedience in engaging in spiritual conversation. The risk he took wasn't his willingness to share but his willingness to invest. Before you get scared off because you think I'm suggesting you become best-friends-forever with everybody you meet, let me assure you there are different levels of investment. Sure, sometimes Jesus calls us to become best friends with someone. Other times, though, He asks us to make simple sacrifices to demonstrate an extra measure of love and care. Philip, the hero of our chapter, doesn't make a huge investment, but he does indeed invest.

Luke, the author of the book of Acts, doesn't give us many details about exactly where Philip is traveling, but we know that at this point in the story, he makes a stop at a mighty revival in the region of Samaria (see Acts 8:5-13). While there, Philip amazed the crowds with miraculous signs, and they paid attention to everything he said. People were being healed, and demons were being cast out. Then suddenly, right in the middle of the whole ordeal, an angel tells Philip to travel south on a different road. But why should he leave when God is using Philip to do amazing miraculous acts and the large crowds are listening to his every word? In most Christians' minds, his evangelism was successful. But, apparently, God wanted something different.

I'm the planning type, the type who hates distractions or interruptions to my schedule, even if they are significant. As a pastor, I experience a lot of these divine interruptions, most of which I tolerate, at best. *This wasn't according to the plan*, I often whine. I wonder if that's how Philip felt when the words of the angel gave him a menial task, an investment in the kingdom of God cleverly disguised as an interruption.

Leaving the excitement of the Samarian revival, Philip follows his new orders and heads south on a dusty road. The text says that the Spirit directed Philip to "go to that chariot and stay near it" (Acts 8:29). In the distance, Philip saw a chariot next to which was a eunuch from Ethiopia reading the book of Isaiah out loud. Philip obeys, but he doesn't just go over and stand by the chariot; Acts says, "Philip *ran* up to the chariot" (Acts 8:30, emphasis added).[2] He made a conscious effort to obey *immediately*. Philip was sent on a major detour, one that could have been misconstrued as inefficient, but he obeyed, nonetheless. And not only did he obey, he obeyed in pretty uncomfortable circumstances.

First off, the revival he was at was, I'm sure, fun and exciting and even somewhat satisfying to his ego. Second, the man reading the Bible was a eunuch. If God had asked me to go hang out with a castrated guy, I might run also, but it would probably be in the other direction. (A eunuch is either a man who's had his genitals cut off at some point or has cut off his genitals himself. You have to wonder what could be going through a person's mind the day they have a brilliant idea like, *Hey, you know, I think I'll cut off my genitals!* Scary. It raises a whole bunch of questions about his masculinity—questions I for one won't be asking. Recently, though, I read that a rugby fan vowed to cut off his genitals if his team, Wales, beat England. The Welsh team pulled off a huge upset over England for the win, and the fan kept his promise. Just another example of someone who takes sports just a little too seriously.)[3]

I find it very interesting that the angel of the Lord didn't say to Philip, "Go witness to the eunuch." Witnessing, as we tend to define it today, is the easy part. I wonder if Philip considered the option of a drive-by witnessing at that point: Go in, spit it out, and head back to Samaria, where the real action was.

But the angel asked him to only stand by the chariot and stay near it. I think there are times when God simply nudges us to "go over to that area and stay there. See what happens." Sometimes the Holy Spirit uses our location to strike up a conversation or be involved in an interaction with others that will have eternal impact. If only we would realize that these God-given opportunities are all around us.

Most of the time when God nudges me to go to a specific location or person or situation, it happens at the most inconvenient time. To turn around and help the man at the corner with the cardboard sign, even though it's rush hour and I'm on my way to work, would seem completely unproductive. And stopping to ask someone who's had a difficult few months how he is really doing would be inconvenient. Every time a distraction such as these comes up, I have the opportunity to risk my own personal schedule and convenience in order to provide value and care and see what God has in store.

After he arrives at the chariot, Philip asks, "Do you understand what you are reading?" The Ethiopian responds by saying, "How can I unless someone explains it to me?" (Acts 8:30-31). The Ethiopian invites him to come and sit in his chariot and engage in conversation about the confusing passage in Isaiah.

It's interesting that Philip started to engage with the man by asking questions. Asking questions is such a great way to start because we are no longer in control of the conversation. When we ask questions—and then shut our mouths long enough to truly listen to the answers—we show others we are willing to invest our time. That's the difference between Philip and Eddie: a willingness (or lack thereof) to invest. Although Eddie asked questions, he certainly didn't shut up long enough to listen to or care about our answers. No dirty mess to clean up. Philip had no idea how big the chariot mess might be, but he grabbed a towel and walked right in.[4]

Of course, God's impact through our obedience always spans further than we could imagine. Clearly, something significant happened between Philip and that eunuch because historians and scholars strongly believe that this Ethiopian was one of the greatest catalysts to the spread of the gospel in Africa.

Protests of Protests

A few days before Easter this year, I read in the local newspaper that a radically fundamental church from the Midwest was coming to our city to protest our government's alleged "pro-gay policies." This church has a reputation of traveling all over the country stirring up controversy and media attention in the name of God, engaging in something their website calls "a unique picketing ministry." The signs they display all over the country are unbelievably offensive, gruesome, and untrue, including signs that read, "God Hates Fags," "God Hates America," and "Thank God for 9/11." This church's message of hatred and judgment was doing more harm than good in our city and in every other city they visited. Rumor had it they

75

were going to show up in front of one of our downtown restaurants, which happened to be owned by the vice mayor of our city.

I drove down to the restaurant with my friend Matt to observe firsthand what would unfold. As the snow fell, I parked my car and walked toward the restaurant wondering, *What the heck am I doing here? How can I make any impact on this situation?* I wasn't going to give these picketers a piece of my mind, nor did I believe I could change their beliefs, but I truly felt that if Jesus were here in the flesh today, He probably would have been down at this restaurant loving and praying, listening, caring, and bandaging up the wounds of those targeted by this church. So, I was convinced that if He would choose to be here, I should do the same.

More and more people began showing up, and an estimated 150 counter-protesters stood out in front of the restaurant when the members from this Midwest church drove up with a police escort and quietly got out of their vehicles. I noticed the presence of the mayor and two city council members and asked what they thought about the entire ordeal. While Matt was off talking with some other people, I approached many of the protesters and simply asked them what they were trying to communicate with their signs. I also felt the need to apologize to the counter-protesters and passersby, assuring them I was convinced there was no possible way Jesus would be standing across the street holding up a "God Hates Fags" sign. Conversation ensued.

During the protest, I happened to look over and lock eyes with a middle-aged African-American woman with a head of dreadlocks that looked like a brown pom-pom. She was drinking coffee to keep warm while she watched the whole ordeal. She smiled at me, and I went over and introduced myself. She said her name was Tina. I asked Tina what she thought about this entire event. I asked her questions like, *"What does this make you think of Christians?" "Do you think all Christians are like this?" "Is this hurtful and painful to you?" "Where is truth in all of this?"* and *"What do you think God thinks about all of this?"*

Tina and I had a delightful conversation, as she told me her opinions and gave me honest answers to all of my questions. She told me about how she volunteered for an organization for homeless teenagers and how she loved serving there every week. She said she just loved those kids, as difficult as they were. She then turned and introduced me to the dreadlocked woman standing next to her, her partner, Janice.

After some pleasantries, Tina asked me that familiar question: "So, what do you do?"

I took a deep breath.

"I'm a pastor," I replied.

"Oh [awkward pause] . . . wow," she said. "That's . . . cool." (By the tone of her voice, I could tell she didn't really think it was all that cool.)

Then she asked me, "What do you think of this whole thing?" I told her why I came and how I did believe that homosexuality was a sin but that just as wrong, if not more, was the hatred this church from the Midwest directed toward people. The entire time, Tina and Janice actually stood there listening and smiling while I shared how my beliefs differed from theirs *and* differed from the protesters' across the street. Surprisingly, they stood there without trying to punch me. I found the whole thing quite interesting—a pastor standing outside in the snow having a delightful conversation with two lesbians about God and Jesus, faith and love. But then I thought that this is what Jesus would be doing, too. He would be standing in the snow right next to us.

After more conversation, Matt joined us and we all went inside the restaurant and got some pizza. When the pizza was gone, we exchanged e-mail addresses and hugs. I tell you, that was a new experience for me—being graciously embraced by two lesbians with genuine hugs. Though our views differed dramatically, I had made two new friends that afternoon and felt like I experienced some real-life evangelism.

For the past several months, my wife and I have regularly met with Tina and Janice to share meals and hike some beautiful Colorado trails. We continue to pray for future opportunities and conversations about God and life and faith with them. And I've realized God has taught me quite a bit since my drive-by witnessing days.

The opportunity God provided for Matt and me was in stark contrast with the protesters' tactics and many other experiences with evangelism I have had. For the protesters, interaction with people was not the goal; there was no investment, no time or effort or desire to get involved in the lives of others. I actually felt sad for them as I watched them stand silently and awkwardly in the snow while people stared at them in confusion. I'm not sure if they expected everyone to read the signs and instantly fall to their knees in repentance or what, but insulting people and then hoping they come to know Jesus is not a fair expectation.

Unlike the protesters and Eddie, and unlike many of us much of the time, Jesus devoted His entire life to investing in people. He took on human flesh to come to earth, walk the dusty roads of Israel, and spend His last few remaining years investing in teenaged fishermen and tax collectors and prostitutes and other lost men and women. He saw the blind, walked alongside paralytics, and touched lepers.

People questioned His motives and wondered if He had completely lost His mind. Why? Because He was doing something very few people are willing to do: giving His life away for others, every day. And like the angel did with Philip, He invites us to do the same.

Going Further

1. When you think of evangelism, what comes to mind? How have your experiences — good and bad — shaped your thoughts on the subject?

2. Have you ever been on the receiving — or giving — end of a drive-by witnessing? How did it make you feel afterward?

3. Name some reasons loving others can be so inconvenient. What does messy love require of us?

4. Some people I know are shocked to hear that I continue to hang out with Tina and Janice. Others are appalled that I would tell them their lifestyle is wrong. Describe the middle ground between condemning and condoning. How can we learn from Jesus' example?

5. In whom is God calling you to invest?

Therefore I will boast all the more gladly about my weaknesses, so that Christ's power may rest on me. This is why, for Christ's sake, I delight in weaknesses, in insults, in hardships, in persecutions, in difficulties. For when I am weak, then I am strong.

— the apostle Paul

Success is never final and failure is never fatal. It's courage that counts.

— George Tilton

Success and failure are both greatly over-rated. But failure gives you a whole lot more to talk about.

— Hildegard Knef

HAVING A NO-GOOD, VERY

5 BAD DAY

JEREMIAH, THE WEEPING PROPHET

ast Company, in their June 2004 issue, featured an article titled "The Thrill of Defeat."[1] The article looked at Pfizer pharmaceutical company, which spends eight billion dollars a year researching and developing new drugs. The most amazing statistic about this company, *Fast Company* points out, is that 96 percent of its efforts in the laboratory end in failure. Most researchers never work on a winning drug their entire career. What a depressing job. (I thought playing baseball was bad. As a hitter, if you fail only two-thirds of the time at the plate, you'll make the All-Star team. In fact, Ted Williams, seen by many as the greatest hitter to ever play the game of baseball, remarkably hit .400 one season, which means he failed 60% of the time.)[2]

Nancy Hutson spent fifteen years in the Pfizer lab working on thirty-five drugs, which cost hundreds of millions of dollars, and not one of them made it to the shelf of your local pharmacy. Not one.[3] But Hutson is now the director of the laboratory at Pfizer. (Yeah, she got a *promotion*. Just doesn't feel quite right, does it?) She oversees all of the efforts of the lab researchers in Research and Development.

83

Pfizer's goal is to cut the failure rate from 96 percent to 92 percent (doubling their success rate) over the next decade. She said, "We have to help researchers understand that only a tiny minority of them—over their entire careers—will ever touch a winning drug. We need our employees to realize that being faithful and focused on our projects in the midst of seemingly insurmountable failure is as important as almost everything that we do."[4] At this drug company, the primary goal is not success but faithful and focused work. Success in the lab is measured by faithfulness (hard work and loyalty to the task), not results. You might think that with a success rate of 4 percent, Pfizer would be on the brink of extinction in the pharmaceutical world, yet Pfizer is the largest pharmaceutical company in the world. Dang.

Worshiping at the Altar of Success

84   In a culture that worships success like nothing else, the way Pfizer functions makes no sense. To us, success *is* results. There's constant pressure to make the grade—to get on the dean's list, get a high-paying job, be recognized in a profession, and get a promotion. There's no doubt our culture values success more than it values faithfulness. Why work hard, be loyal, or pay your dues when you can become a star or filthy rich in minutes by cutting corners or cheating? I'm willing to bet that if you took a poll and asked a few dozen people on the street which they would choose, being successful or faithful, success would win hands down.

And it'd be nice to think that Christians don't feel this way, but we often do. The drive for success, although the definitions may change a bit in a Christian environment, is a strong temptation in the church, too. Pastors feel pressure to grow their congregations in attendance and giving. Missionaries feel pressure to report back to their supporters stories of conversions and tangible ministry accomplishments. Talking about this over coffee with my friends Bob and Tom, both missionaries themselves, I learned there is a temptation for missionaries to want to exaggerate stories and reports in order to look successful and worthy of receiving continual support. When have you ever received a support letter from a missionary that reported complete and utter failure? Something like, "Well, in the past three years of work here on the mission field, we have seen no success whatsoever. Nothing. No one has come to Christ as a result of our work, people have been unreceptive to the gospel, and we're completely discouraged. Thank you for your ongoing financial support." That just doesn't happen.

We desperately crave success not only because we question our own worth if we fail but also because we know our culture, Christian or not, constantly sizes us up according to its standards for success.

When we aren't successful, we wonder what happened and where we went wrong. It's tempting to quit, try something new, and attempt to be successful somewhere else. Accepting the possibility of failure and sticking to a task regardless is part of what it means to risk big.

A Biblical Failure

There was once a guy who lost at everything he did. His name was Jeremiah, and he's got an entire Old Testament book written about his life. He was called to be a prophet to the nations, a human mouthpiece through whom God communicated important truths to His people. Jeremiah's life and struggles are shown on the pages of our Bibles in great detail, in greater depth than any other prophet, so it's interesting to note that his reports contain mostly stories of failure. I highly doubt you or I would even consider supporting him financially. Eugene Peterson describes Jeremiah this way:

85

Everything that could go wrong *did* go wrong. And
Jeremiah was in the middle of it all, sticking it out, praying
and preaching, suffering and striving, writing and believing.
He lived through crushing storms of hostility and furies of
bitter doubt.[5]

Here's the story of why Jeremiah felt like such a loser. He was called
by God to be a divine spokesman to the people in his country. God
spoke to him and told him that He had picked out Jeremiah spe-
cifically for this task. He said, "Before I formed you in the womb I
knew you, before you were born I set you apart; I appointed you as
a prophet to the nations" (Jeremiah 1:5).

"Tell them to repent and I will protect you," God said. "You
warn them that if they don't turn, there will be great destruction." And Jeremiah did exactly what God asked him to do. For
years he called and petitioned the people to repentance, and
they were completely unresponsive. The people were comfortable, apathetic, secure, nonchalant, and arrogant, and they
turned their backs on God completely. As Jeremiah's pleas for
Israel's repentance grew more strenuous, the people grew more
tired of him. They became irritated and scorned him. They beat
him up, dragged him into the center of town, and put him in
the stocks so everyone could humiliate him. Scholars believe
they put him near one of the main entrances into the temple so
everyone could see him on their way in and out of worship.

Jeremiah struggled so much that he is known as "the weeping
prophet."

It Only Gets Worse

The people from Jeremiah's hometown and his family not only beat
him but also wanted to kill him for his prophesies. He complained to

God, "All my friends are waiting for me to slip" (Jeremiah 20:10). And the religious leaders said, "This man should be sentenced to death because he has prophesied against this city" (Jeremiah 26:11).

The king of Israel at the time, King Zedekiah, arrested Jeremiah and told him to shut up and get out. Jeremiah took it pretty hard. He needed some therapy, or at least a long vacation or something.

In Scripture, Jeremiah reflected on his life, something that is pretty easy to do when you experience a great deal of loss and failure. Finally, he decided he was going to tell God exactly how he felt. He was going to give Him a piece of his mind. Jeremiah was upset and frustrated and wasn't afraid to show it. He started by saying,

> O LORD, you deceived me, and I was deceived;
>   you overpowered me and prevailed.
> I am ridiculed all day long;
>   everyone mocks me.
> Whenever I speak, I cry out
>   proclaiming violence and destruction.
> So the word of the LORD has brought me
>   insult and reproach all day long. (Jeremiah 20:7-8)[6]

Did you notice that first line? He called God a liar: "You deceived me, God. You lied to me." Those are pretty audacious words to share with Someone who has the power to strike you dead at any moment. But I suppose that by then, the threat of death was something he had gotten somewhat comfortable with. After Jeremiah spent plenty of time complaining, he added,

> But if I say, "I will not mention him
>   or speak any more in his name,"
> his word is in my heart like a fire,
>   a fire shut up in my bones.
> I am weary of holding it in;
>   indeed, I cannot. (Jeremiah 20:9)

Even though all these terrible things have happened, confusing him about why God would allow all of this pain and heartache in the midst of his obedience, shouldn't he be honored and blessed for his behavior? He admits he'll be willing to obey anyway, because he can't *not* do it. And then he proclaims, in a manner similar to King David in his most grateful psalms,

> Sing to the LORD!
>   Give praise to the LORD!
> He rescues the life of the needy
>   from the hands of the wicked. (Jeremiah 20:13)

In the midst of his terrible circumstances, the confused and angry prophet picked himself up, brushed off the dirt, and told the people to repent—*again*. But, as things seem to do in Jeremiah's life, they only got worse. Some rebellious Israelites decided to dump him in a deep cistern and leave him to die.

Cisterns

When I studied in Israel, I lived in an old architectural structure that sits at the top of Mount Zion in Jerusalem. Underneath the buildings of the college are cisterns. One day my roommates and I stumbled upon an old map in the library that detailed the exact locations of each cistern under the school. We managed to discover their locations and climbed into all but one of them throughout the semester. One evening my three roommates lowered me down into one through a small opening just wide enough for my shoulders to fit through. As a joke, they decided to put the manhole cover back on and leave. It was dark and freaky and cold and lonely. My mind started playing tricks on me; I started seeing things in the water. Strangely enough, I had been studying Jeremiah in my quiet times those days. I remember thinking, as I was shivering and terrified in my swimsuit, *This must be just a hint of what Jeremiah felt like when he was in the cistern.*

If it weren't for Jeremiah's friends finding him and pulling him out, he would have died in the bottom of that cistern. Fortunately, for me, too, after what felt like an eternity, my roommates—I'd like to call them my *former* friends—finally returned and rescued me.

Israel's Trail of Tears

Jeremiah demonstrated a truly supernatural measure of faithfulness in spite of his failure. He chose to speak a message that the people didn't want to hear, but their interest in his message had no consequence because God's call was God's call—period. He continued to share the message God had appointed him to share: "If you don't listen to what I say and turn from your ways, foreign armies will come and carry us all off into exile and captivity" (my paraphrase).

And sure enough, he was right. A mighty foreign army marched into Jerusalem. The king of the enemy, Nebuchadnezzar, invaded the country. The city was under siege for almost three years. Nebuchadnezzar killed the children of Zedekiah, king of Israel, right in front of him. And immediately following, Nebuchadnezzar gouged Zedekiah's eyes out so that the last thing he saw was the murder of his own children. In 587 BC, the Babylonian army carried off more than four thousand Jews from Judah into captivity, including the blind king and the weeping prophet, making them march six hundred miles to the north. It was the Trail of Tears of biblical times. The city of Jerusalem, once standing in splendor, was laid in a silent pile of burning destruction. A once thriving city of God was left deserted, destroyed and in disgrace, and King Zedekiah eventually died in exile.

Jeremiah is a perfect example of someone who had every excuse in the book to pull the plug and give up on God. By most standards, his ministry was a complete failure. All his work, and nothing happened.

No one repented. Looking at Jeremiah's life kind of makes working at Pfizer sound appealing.

A Biblical Winner

After the Jews returned from exile, God raised up a prophet named Haggai. God had a job for Haggai, but contrary to Jeremiah, he was thoroughly successful. People listened to his message, repenting from their evil ways and turning their lives around. The temple in Jerusalem was rebuilt during Haggai's ministry, and overall he checked off quite a number of impressive duties on his Prophet Checklist. By all measures, he would have been named Prophet of the Century and had his face on the front cover of *Christianity Today.*

The Definition of Success

90 The stories of Jeremiah and Haggai prompt an important question: What does it truly mean to be successful, and by whose standard? Everything in us wants to turn every project and job and assignment into a Haggai-type deal. Haggai's results are more attractive to us because, well, who wants to fail? But we have to be prepared for a Jeremiah experience.

It's important for us to understand how God responded to each prophet. Sure, the world's response is easy to predict because God called both men to do a job and they had completely different results. So, of course, if these guys were CEOs instead of prophets, we know who would get the raise and who would get canned. And we might think God would have reacted the same way: pat Haggai on the back and "reassign" Jeremiah to something a bit less challenging. But despite their very different results, both prophets heard the same thing from God: "Good job! You were faithful to the task."

One of my favorite quotes of all time is from Mother Teresa. She said, "God does not call us to be successful; He calls us to be faithful."[7] It's sometimes hard to believe that God is not concerned about our success, even though almost everyone else in the world is. But it's true. When God asks us to be obedient, He doesn't often share the intended end result with us. The result is irrelevant because God's desire is for us to be faithful to the task whether or not we succeed according to our own standards.

What if God, for some weird reason, put you in a situation in which you were failing left and right like Jeremiah or those lab researchers at Pfizer? For instance, what if you were rejected from every college you applied to and forced to attend a local community college you had no interest in attending? Or what if you finished graduate school and looked for a position that fit your education level only to find your sole job offer from a coffee shop? What if you chose to pursue a woman you sensed to be your future wife and she wanted nothing to do with you? What if this really was a part of His will for your life? Would you be okay with that?

91

Scripture tells us that if we are obedient, we won't hear God say to us, "Well done, good and *successful* servant," but instead, "Well done, good and *faithful* servant." The difference between the sentences is found in one word, but its significance is huge. I think it's important to point out that success is not inherently a bad thing. Remember, God was the one who brought success to Haggai in the first place.[8] But success is not our goal; God's plans for us are the goal. And let's not forget: God is the very definition of faithfulness. He'll take care of things, but it'll just be in His own unique, often-confusing way.

The Faithfulness of Mr. Holland

One of my favorite movies is *Mr. Holland's Opus*. It isn't an action film, it wasn't a summer blockbuster, but it communicates a message of faithfulness over success like almost no other movie I've ever seen. Glenn Holland, played by Richard Dreyfuss, has big dreams. He desires to be known as a great musician and a composer by creating an opus that would make him one of the elite American contemporary composers of his day. But he needs to provide some financial stability for his family, so he reluctantly takes a position teaching music at a high school in small-town America for a couple of years.

He becomes overwhelmed by his teaching job and has very little time to work on his masterpiece. He finds out quickly that this was not what he had signed up for. He works long hours, he deals with difficult students, and the band sounds awful. He is frustrated by the failure, bad attitudes, and poor skills of his students. But despite his apparent lack of success, he believes this is where he's supposed to be, so he is faithful to his students for three decades. After thirty years, the school board cuts the music department budget and Mr. Holland is forced into retirement.

As Mr. Holland, his wife, and his now grown-up son, Cole, are cleaning out the last of his belongings from his old classroom, they hear music coming from the auditorium. If you've seen the movie, you know that the event to follow is a tearjerker. I'm teary-eyed just writing this right now (but then again, I am a pretty sappy guy to begin with). His students have planned a surprise assembly in his honor, in which they played the opus he never had published, one that never had been performed but undoubtedly would have brought him fame and fortune and success. The surprise emcee of the event is the state governor, who many years prior was a discouraged clarinet player in his music class. She says, "We are your symphony, Mr. Holland. We are the melodies and the notes of your opus, and we are the music of your life." The room is full of people who communicate their appreciation: *We know that you could have been famous and successful, but you chose to be faithful.* The amazing thing is that in his faithfulness, Mr. Holland had an influence far greater than any riches or fame could have brought him.

God may call some of you to be a Haggai, and He may call some of you to be a Jeremiah. But God's desire for your life, no matter who you are or what you do, isn't success in the eyes of the world but risking potential failure for faithfulness to Him.

Going Further

1. Why is it we strive so hard for success?

2. Describe a "cistern experience" of your own, when you felt utterly alone and like a failure. Why did you feel the way you did?

3. "Jeremiah is a perfect example of someone who had every excuse in the book to pull the plug and give up on God." When have you been tempted to give up on God and not be faithful? For what reason?

4. How do you define success? Where do you think that definition came from?

5. Think about Mother Teresa's quote, "God does not call us to be successful; He calls us to be faithful." What implications does that have on your life? How does that alter your thoughts about God?

6. What can you do to develop the willingness to risk failure in order to be faithfully obedient to God?

We must be willing to let go of the life we have planned, so as to accept the life that is waiting for us.

— Joseph Campbell

The hardest part of anything is the beginning, and the second hardest part is letting go when it's the end.

— E. Fritz

6 LETTING GO OF YOUR PEANUTS

THE RICH YOUNG RULER

One of history's greatest purposes is to help us learn from others' mistakes. So, while most of this book draws encouragement from people in Scripture who took risks for God, this chapter does the opposite. We'll learn from a man who *should* have taken a risk but chose not to and had to live with the consequences. This man chose not to abandon his material security, his possessions, in order to follow Christ.

The story, told by Luke, revolved around a conversation between Jesus and this young man, who wasn't just any average guy. This man had three things going for him: He was rich, he was young, and he was a ruler. This man's economic status fell within the top 1 to 2 percent of the entire country. He was also young, and in that culture it was rare that one would be both young and rich at the same time. And the fact that he was also a ruler was even rarer. We don't know what exactly he ruled, but we can bet it was pretty important. Just to tell you how atypical this was, it would be like a twenty-six-year-old becoming the new CEO of Apple. This guy was one of the most privileged members of society. Today he probably would be on the cover of *Forbes* and his house might be featured on *Cribs*.

The Interaction with Jesus

We know that this young man respected Jesus, because upon seeing Him, the man ran to Him. Rich people never ran in that day—running was for the lower class. But this man, somehow, trusted Jesus and knew that He had some authority.

When he reached Jesus, he asked, "Good teacher, what must I do to inherit eternal life?" (Luke 18:18). Jesus responded in a way common to rabbis: He answered the question with another question.

"Why do you call me good?" Jesus asked without expecting an answer from the man. "No one is good—except God alone" (verse 19). Jesus was not saying the man was wrong in his statement; He was questioning what he meant by the title "good teacher." He was challenging the man's view of who God was.

Bar Mitzvah: Dancing, Candy, and Manhood

Jesus then answered the rich man's question: "You know the commandments: 'Do not commit adultery, do not murder, do not steal, do not give false testimony, honor your father and mother'" (Luke 18:20). He rattled off the fifth through the ninth commandments, the section of the Ten Commandments that addresses how we relate to one another. It is interesting what the man's response was: "All these I have kept since I was a boy" (verse 21). And in that culture, you ceased to be a boy at your bar mitzvah.

Bar mitzvahs happened, and still do today, for thirteen-year-old Jewish boys. I remember being at the Western Wall in Jerusalem and watching one of these bar mitzvah celebrations just a few feet away from me. A young boy gleefully jumped around as he held up a giant Torah scroll while older men—probably grandpas and uncles and cousins—danced around him and women threw candy at him. When the dancing died down, he did something he had never done before: He read from the Torah scroll. At the time, I found the whole ordeal rather odd. (If I remember correctly, my thirteenth birthday was quite different from this. I think my parents ordered pizza, and my friends and I watched a movie.)

The bar mitzvah is the most important birthday of a Jewish male's life. It is the point from which he is held entirely accountable and responsible for all of his actions. At his bar mitzvah, he acknowledges that now, officially, he is an adult. When the rich young ruler claimed he had kept all of the commandments since he was a boy, he claimed he had obeyed them since the time he celebrated his bar mitzvah. That's a long time to keep all those commandments (unless he turned thirteen yesterday). This guy was *good!*

99

In Mark 10, a parallel account of this story, we read an interesting phrase: "Jesus looked at him and loved him" (verse 21). What a striking phrase. We know that Jesus wasn't just nonchalantly answering this man's question; Jesus truly cared about him. That makes the weight of his next response more acceptable, because Jesus didn't arbitrarily ask something from the man—He truly wanted this man to follow Him and experience true life. Jesus said, "Go, sell everything you have and give to the poor, and you will have treasure in heaven. Then come, follow me" (verse 21).

Wait. How does getting rid of all his stuff relate to eternal life? Jesus seemed to think there's a major connection. During His ministry, Jesus spoke more about the topic of money than about love, grace, salvation, and serving. He talked more about money than about heaven and hell combined. It's because when Jesus said, "Where your treasure is, there your heart will be also" (Matthew 6:21), He meant He could tell how devoted a person is to God by what that person treasured most. So all the other things, such as service and grace, would follow a heart totally devoted to God. In this case, Jesus had a hunch this rich young ruler treasured his money above all else.

Jesus does not call every person to do what He called this man to do. Being a follower of God doesn't revolve around works, like how much we give or how much we don't give (despite what those strange televangelists say). Jesus was not giving a universal command; He was giving a universal test. He was testing the rich young ruler to discover the attachments to his heart. It was a control test: He was asking, "What controls you and keeps you from wholeheartedly following Christ?" For the ruler, it was money. For you, it could be any number of things.

Control or Freedom?

After Jesus had told the man to go sell everything, the man's face fell. The man went away sad "because he had great wealth" (Mark 10:22). The man walked away. He may have been good at keeping a few commandments, but when the rubber met the road, and following God meant *real* sacrifice, this guy folded.

The rich young ruler ruled over many things but not over his own stuff. His stuff ruled him. How sad that his greatest downfall was money. The rich young ruler "was holding on tight to a lot of things, and not about to let go" (verse 22, MSG). Jesus knew that if this young man's money controlled him, the man couldn't surrender his whole self, which is exactly what Jesus desired of him. The risk about surrender is that you lose everything else, and for the rich young ruler, that wasn't acceptable.

It's no wonder Jesus spoke so much—and so strongly—about rich people. I believe that Jesus understood the seductive power of money. Think about it: With money, you can control almost anything, can't you? If you cut the tie of money, what are you left with?

Rob Bell, a pastor in Grand Rapids, Michigan, once said, "God doesn't want our money. He wants our freedom."[1] Jesus desires that we live free lives, lives of purpose, lives that lack oppression and slavery. He wants us to be free. True freedom doesn't come from having enough wealth to live a worry-free life, although we all dream of such; true freedom comes when we surrender our desire for riches, or whatever else controls us, and offer everything to Christ.

Camels and Needles

Jesus said, "How hard it is for the rich to enter the kingdom of God" (Mark 10:23). He had the boldness to make this statement within earshot of one of the country's richest men. In America, we don't like to tick off rich people, but Jesus had no problem speaking the truth even if it hurt. We're told the disciples were amazed by His words. Jesus took the comment even further: "It is easier for a camel to go through the eye of a needle than for a rich man to enter the kingdom of God" (verse 25).

This phrase is a hyperbole, a literary device that uses exaggeration to drive home a point.[2] Camels were the largest animals found in first-century Palestine, and the smallest opening known in the first century was the eye of a needle. So obviously, Jesus' statement was not meant to be taken literally. He was taking the two extremes: the largest mammal and the smallest opening. If Jesus had meant this statement to be taken literally, there would have been one mutilated camel. The point? Money is the strongest force that keeps people from surrendering to Jesus. This is not surprising to any of us, I'm sure, because we know what it feels like to hold tightly to our possessions.

Surprisingly, studies have shown that the more money we have, the less generous we become. One organization reports that U.S. Christians give proportionately less today than they did during the Great Depression.[3] People get flustered and offended when talk moves toward the subject of money in church because they think all people want is to get into their wallet. But we've got to understand that there is a deeper issue here, and it's not about our wallet—it's about our heart, and ultimately about our freedom.

At the end of the story of the rich young ruler, the disciples became even more amazed and asked, "Who then can be saved?" (verse 26). They were wondering, *If the rich man, whom God has blessed with wealth, cannot get into heaven, then who can? If the top of the ladder cannot get in, then is there even a fightin' chance for the rest of us?* Peter, in his typical foot-in-mouth fashion, boldly stepped up and said, "We have left everything to follow you!" (verse 28). Jesus went on to assure Peter that he was right—that he and the rest of the guys did leave everything and would be rewarded for that. Jesus assured them they would not be forgotten.

I've wondered about what Jesus said to Peter. Would He say that statement about *my* life? Can you say you have left *everything* to follow Jesus?

The Last 5 Percent

A few years ago, I was at a conference where Bill Hybels, senior pastor of Willow Creek Community Church, said something that hit me like a ton of bricks: "It is easy to give God 95 percent of our lives, but it's the last 5 percent that is the most difficult. And 95 percent commitment to Christ is 5 percent short."[4]

He's right. Most of us are able to give God most of our lives, because, after all, we don't have the brainpower to control everything (although some of us still try). But there's always something that binds us, that last 5 percent that we cling to with a white-knuckle grip. Maybe for you, the last 5 percent isn't about money as it was for the rich young ruler. Maybe it's about your future plans, your significant other, your job, or an addictive habit that you just can't imagine giving up. Or maybe you can't give up your craving to manage your reputation and what others think of you. Because it involves the hard stuff that you just don't *want* to relinquish, letting go of the last five percent requires the greatest risk.

When Peter said, "We have given up everything," he was talking percentage points. Jesus agreed. "You're right. You're 100 percenters and you will not be forgotten for that" (see Mark 10:29-31). That last 5 percent of control is the risky stuff, because letting go of what we hold dearer than God is a painful process strewn with attempted discipline and sacrifice. John Ortberg once said that people don't drift into full devotion to God; it takes a committed decision to do it. It takes blood, sweat, and tears—total devotion and a decision that says following Jesus is most important.

103

In the book of Acts, followers of Jesus had committed themselves to an unprecedented movement called the Way: "All the believers were together and had everything in common. Selling their possessions and goods, they gave to anyone as he had need" (Acts 2:44-45). A few chapters later, these passionate followers of Jesus did it again. "All the believers were one in heart and mind. No one claimed that any of his possessions was his own, but they shared everything they had. . . . There were no needy persons among them. For from time to time those who owned land or houses sold them, brought the money from the sales and put it at the apostles' feet, and it was distributed to anyone as he had need" (Acts 4:32,34-35). They were people who let go of control of their lives—including their finances—and let the Holy Spirit control them.

The rich young ruler's risk involved having to rely completely on God for his finances, and he couldn't do it. He just couldn't do it. He gave God 95 percent, but the cords of the 5 percent were wrapped so tightly around his finances that he just couldn't let go. I don't know what God is asking you to surrender, but you can feel free to ask Him. And we can learn from the ruler that walking away is a choice that will lead us to only incompleteness—a lack of true life.

Clenching Your Peanuts

Last summer I heard a story about a group of scientific researchers in Indonesia who wanted to do laboratory tests on monkeys. In order to capture the monkeys for their tests, they would shoot the monkeys with tranquilizer guns, instantly putting them to sleep with one shot, which would make it possible for the researchers to perform an assortment of medical tests. But there was a problem: When the researchers shot the tranquilizers, the monkeys, who were perched in extremely tall trees, would instantly fall asleep and free-fall to their death.[5]

In pursuit of a less destructive way to capture the monkeys, the researchers stumbled onto a five-hundred-year-old practice. They hollowed out a gourd, like a squash or pumpkin, about the size of a basketball, and created an opening in the top about the size of a silver dollar. At the opposite end of the gourd, they attached a long rope. One researcher stood in the bushes holding the rope while another stood with a burlap sack a few yards away. A third researcher would get the attention of the monkey up in the tree, and as the monkey watched, the researcher would drop peanuts—irresistible to monkeys—into the gourd. A few moments later, the monkey would climb down the tree toward the gourd and stick his hand in the hole, which was just big enough to fit the monkey's wrist. The monkey would reach for the peanuts, and at that point, you've got yourself a monkey.

The monkeys then had a choice: let go of the peanuts, or be captured by the researchers. In every case, the researchers would pull out their burlap sack and easily capture the monkeys without harm because the monkeys, under any circumstance, wouldn't let go of the peanuts. Of course, if they would just let go of the peanuts, their hands would slide right through the hole and they could easily outrun the researchers. We are those monkeys.

How often we forfeit our freedom because we refuse to surrender something we greatly desire. We choose things, insignificant things, that often become an obsession, only to realize we're still missing something better. The choice is yours. You can hold on tight to the last 5 percent, whatever those peanuts happen to be for you, or you can gain true life by releasing that control and running toward freedom.

Going Further

1. What are the sacrifices of total surrender to Christ? What are the gains?

2. It has been said that the danger in owning things is that they very easily can own you. Is there anything that owns you?

3. Bill Hybels said, "Ninety-five percent commitment to Christ is 5 percent short." Why does God require our 100 percent commitment to Him? Why is anything less than 5 percent not enough?

4. What is your last 5 percent? What is it that you believe God truly wants you to surrender? What might be His motive behind His request?

Confrontation is not a dirty word. Sometimes it's the best kind of journalism as long as you don't confront people just for the sake of a confrontation.

—Don Hewitt

It is not the critic who counts; not the man who points out how the strong man stumbled or where the doer of deeds could have done them better. The credit belongs to the man who is actually in the arena; whose face is marred by dust and sweat and blood; who errs and comes up short again and again . . . who knows the great enthusiasms, the great devotions, and spends himself in a worthy cause; who at the least knows in the end the triumph of high achievement; and who, at the worst, if he fails, at least fails while daring greatly, so that his place shall never be with those cold and timid souls who know neither victory nor defeat.

—Teddy Roosevelt

7 SPEAKING UP WHEN YOU WANT TO SHUT UP

NATHAN, A PROPHET TO KING DAVID

few months ago, I spent a restful afternoon reading a book in a comfortable, overstuffed chair at Barnes & Noble. Everything was calm and peaceful, with soft music humming in the background and my chai tea still hot, until suddenly the guy sitting next to me answered his cell phone and ended up in a long, loud conversation, never moving from his chair. Apparently, nobody had taught this guy about using his inside voice. His inconsiderate intrusion quickly turned my calm mood sour.

I wanted to tell him to shut up because everyone within three city blocks could hear his conversation involving way too much information about Aunt Maria's health problems. But I chickened out. It was probably better in the long run that I didn't say something, because I doubt I would have been polite. But that experience made me think about how confrontation is an issue for me in general; it's something I don't exactly enjoy doing. Some people like confrontation, but the majority of us avoid it at almost all costs. Most of the time, whether you're on the giving or receiving end, confrontation is awkward and even painful.

Sometimes I think it would be less painful to have my front teeth pulled without Novocain.

Instances involving confrontation can range from insignificant—for instance, you're out to lunch with your boss and a group of important clients, and you realize your boss has a big, honkin' piece of broccoli stuck between his front teeth, and you're thinking, *Do I tell him and embarrass him, or do I not tell him and chance him being mad at me for not saying anything?*—to the other end of the spectrum, serious. Of course, the serious circumstances are the ones we'll address in this chapter because those require a greater deal of risk. And although it's risky because it forces us to stop being comfortable and even jeopardize a relationship, confrontation is something Scripture calls us to do.[1]

110 There's one particular Bible story about a man named Nathan, who risked his life by confronting someone pretty important in a very serious situation. The account is found in 2 Samuel chapters 11–12. At the time, Israel's government was established as a monarchy, and on the throne sat one of the greatest kings in history: King David.

One evening, David lounged on a high place of his palace for some fresh Middle Eastern air, and scanning the city, he saw a young woman bathing. David knew that the woman, Bathsheba, was totally off-limits. She was the wife of Uriah, a loyal soldier in the army protecting King David's kingdom. But David ordered his servants to bring Bathsheba up to his place anyway because she was gorgeous and he couldn't resist.

That night, David commited adultery with Bathsheba, and as a result, Bathsheba became pregnant.[2] Out of panic, David attempted to cover up what had happened. As Bathsheba's husband, Uriah, was out fighting to protect Israel's borders, David sent a message ordering him to return home and spend some time with his wife. David assumed that during Uriah's time home, he and Bethsheba would do that thing married people do, and then Bathsheba's child would appear to be Uriah's, simple as that.

But the plan backfired. Uriah, being a loyal soldier in David's army, couldn't justify going home and taking time off when the rest of his fellow soldiers were out fighting. So, he went home to Jerusalem but didn't have fun and sleep with his wife. David soon realized his plan was unraveling. As a last-ditch effort, he sent a letter to the commander ordering that Uriah be moved to the front lines, where the battle raged the fiercest, and where he would surely (conveniently) die. The commander obeyed his orders, and Uriah was killed in battle, as David had hoped.[3] David, the greatest king ever to live, twisted himself into a web of sin. He not only committed adultery but he also lied and then murdered one of his most loyal men.[4]

So, where does Nathan come into this story? Nathan was a prophet, and one of his more difficult assignments was to confront the king of Israel about his sin. Obedient to God's call, Nathan approached King David and told him a parable. The story goes that in a certain town lived a wealthy man who had lots of cattle and sheep. In the same town, there was also a very poor man who had only one ewe, which he treated like a daughter. The farmer slept with his lamb at night, petted it, and cared for it, and even let it drink of his cup.

A traveler came to visit the rich man, so the rich man served him dinner. But instead of slaughtering one of his own sheep or cattle, he stole the little lamb that belonged to the poor man and killed it for the traveler's meal. Upon hearing the tragedy of this story, David became angry and said, "As surely as the LORD lives, the man who did this deserves to die! He must pay for that lamb four times over, because he did such a thing and had no pity" (2 Samuel 12:5-6). David was wise enough to make the correct judgment about the situation but not wise enough to recognize that Nathan was speaking about David's own life.[5]

After David's outrage, Nathan uttered probably the most courageous sentence he would ever say: "You are the man!" (2 Samuel 12:7). (Obviously, Nathan wasn't telling David "you da man" but was accusing him of sin. He probably wished he could do the former, since it'd be a lot easier than accusing the king of Israel of being a murderer.) Nathan went on to give David a divine message from God: that he had done evil in the eyes of God by slaying Uriah and taking Bethsheba as his own. And Nathan told him there would be calamity and severe consequences in his family line for what he had done.

When Nathan was finished with his message from God, he had no idea what David's response would be. Maybe he'd become even more furious. He might deny the accusation and focus on semantics like "it depends on what your definition of 'is' is" or wave his finger and say, "I did not have sexual relations with that woman."

Or maybe he would order Nathan killed with a snap of his fingers.

But David's response was nothing short of amazing. He confessed, "I have sinned against the LORD" (2 Samuel 12:13). Later David wrote an honest confession to God, known as Psalm 51.

Confrontation is rarely fun. I've always imagined that when Nathan received this call from God, he wasn't exactly thrilled. It would have been easy for Nathan to claim he couldn't go before such an important man and do such a politically incorrect thing.

Maybe you can think of a time when you should have confronted somebody but avoided doing so, using rationalizations such as:

112

I don't want to rock the boat.

I don't want to make somebody mad if I don't have to.

Who am I to judge? I mean, I've done this before.

He wouldn't listen to me even if I did tell him.

It might ruin our friendship.

There might be friction.

She'd just think I am an overly sensitive drama queen or something.

When faced with an opportunity for confrontation, we usually want to turn our heads and ignore it. I've been in situations in which I was absolutely convinced that even if I confronted someone in the best way possible, he still wouldn't care or he would flip out. But that's not the point. Just because we're scared to confront someone, our rationalizations won't change the fact that this person has offended God and that God wants us to be the bearer of that news.

113

Of course, confrontation can quickly turn sour when we act without a call from God, or, probably worse, with a feigned call from God. Many people have said to me, "God told me to say it," but I end up hearing less of a prophecy and more of a joke. Like every risk we take, awareness of God's direct involvement is pretty crucial. And when God's involved, we have to believe that He's planning on working it out. But God's taking care of the situation doesn't mean our friends or colleagues will love us for our admonishment. They may hate us forever, and we just have to deal with that possibility. Nonetheless, it's not our job to change their mind or behavior. But it *is* our job to be faithful and do the right thing, even if it is hard.

I remember one particular opportunity for confrontation. In college, there was a guy on my wing in Wengatz Hall at Taylor University, a Christian college, who was involved in a behavior I knew wasn't right—and so did he. This guy was stubborn and apathetic and had a reputation for thinking he was just too cool (you know those guys). After sensing God's desire for me to confront him, I thought, *Why would I ever confront him on this issue? He doesn't give a rip about anything, and he definitely won't care what I think.* But after my friends nudged me to obey, I reluctantly walked down to his room, the knot in my stomach getting tighter with each step. I was convinced this would be a complete waste of time and that in the long run he would hate me for it. What little respect he may have had for me would be completely gone.

When I finally arrived at his door, he invited me in. In my most calm tone of voice, I confronted him. I was so nervous that I was shaking and my voice was cracking and my pits were sweaty. I just waited for him to tell me to shut up and mind my own business, but he never did. In fact, he listened intently to what I said. And after a long pause he looked up and said something that truly shocked me: "You're right. I shouldn't be doing this. Thanks for talking to me about it." We ended up talking for a few more minutes. He expressed his desire to change and considered out loud a possible plan to adjust his attitude and behavior.

After our conversation, I walked back down the hall toward my room with my jaw dragging on the carpet. I shut the door, plopped down on our shaggy, yellow eight-foot couch (which my roommate and I affectionately called "The Twinkie") and began to cry. I had doubted that the most powerful Being in the universe could work in this situation. And as tears rolled down my cheeks (like I said, I'm a sappy guy), I asked God to forgive me for underestimating Him and thinking He wasn't powerful enough to work in that situation.

More times than not, however, I have ignored God's call to confront. But I have learned something about what happens when we don't obey, because I have been on the other end of non-confrontation. On several occasions, I have heard, through the grapevine in my community of faith, that certain people left our church because they thought my teaching style was awful or I wasn't biblically based or I was a two-faced leader. But when I had asked the people why they were leaving, they had simply said God was calling them elsewhere.[6] They swept the truth under the rug, hoping it would go away. They ignored the elephant in the room and hoped I wouldn't see it. I *did* discover it, however, and it wounded me. Knowing they avoided a confrontation has actually hurt me because they lied and talked behind my back and didn't help a single thing. When God calls us to confront, it's not just for our own health. He has bigger things in mind, like the fact that He's taking care of the entire body of Christ, and in order to do so, He asks for our help. How can we help Him if we won't be true to each other? Where's the risk in skirting truth?

115

Can you imagine if Jesus would have avoided confrontation? It would have been much safer, to be sure. He could have easily been chummy with Pharisees and Caesars and sinners and disciples. He could have been the nice, cool guy, always telling the men that they're tough and manly and complimenting ladies on how cute their dress is (even though it was actually too frumpy and totally the wrong season). Jesus embraced confrontation—not flippant confrontation but confrontation that served God and His kingdom. Jesus was as politically incorrect as they come.

The Lord Jesus and the prophet Nathan serve as our biblical inspiration to care not about political correctness but about telling the truth in obedience to God. They aren't teaching us to seek out opportunities to pick a fight, but instead they inspire us to seek

out truth and right living and defend it when it is being attacked
(see Matthew 5:9).

The Lion of the Transvaal

Tom, my South African friend, once told me about a pastor in a
region of South Africa called the Transvaal. This pastor was so well
known for being a bold man that he acquired the nickname "The
Lion of the Transvaal." The Lion never shied away from confrontation. Tom told me one particular story about a time when The
Lion stepped up to the podium at the end of a church service and
made one last announcement before dismissing the congregation.
He called to the front a couple who had been in the congregation
for quite some time. The couple did not expect this, so needless to
say they were shocked when The Lion put his arms around them
and told the congregation this would be the last time the couple
would attend the church. The Lion explained that the couple had
been involved in some serious and ongoing gossip. Though they
had been confronted several times, the couple refused to stop
their behavior. "Therefore," The Lion said, "they will no longer be
allowed at our church. So, before they leave tonight, make sure
you tell them good-bye."

While I don't admire The Lion's tactlessness, I do have to admire his
willingness to confront. I believe that The Lion can teach us to be
unafraid of confronting others with the purpose of serving Christ.[7]

We have all been on each side of confrontation. When we are
confronted, as hard as it is, we are called to put ourselves in a posture
of humility, just as David did. Even if the people confronting us
don't make sense, or even if you feel that their confrontation is in
obedience not to God but rather to their emotions, be humble
and listen.

Last summer I was on an airplane with my wife. Before takeoff, she asked me to put her bag into the overhead bin. Instead of helping, I just brushed her off rudely and returned to reading my book. I figured she could handle sitting through the relatively short flight with her bag at her feet. Plus, my seatbelt was already fastened and I was comfortable.

I returned to my book without a thought until I heard sniffles. I realized that instead of loving and serving her in a small way, like I had promised to do in my vows on our wedding day, I had been disrespectful to her and it left her hurt and frustrated, rightfully so. "Sometimes," she said, "you have such a hard time serving people."

She nailed me right between the eyes, and I had no comeback, no excuse, no defense—because she was exactly right. A simple opportunity for me to serve my wife with a thirty-second task, and I had been unwilling to do it. Her words stung at the time, but I'm glad she confronted me. It reminded me that my selfishness can truly hurt others. She showed me that I have a long way to go to truly serving as a husband and a follower of Christ needs to.

Megan demonstrated to me why we confront in the first place. Confrontation helps us grow as a community to be shaped more like Jesus. We aren't helping anything if we ignore our brothers' and sisters' lives just because we don't think it's our business. Think about all the people you know:

Your roommate who sleeps with his girlfriend.

Your friend who smokes pot.

Your pastor who treats his wife like dirt.

Your friend who tells inappropriate jokes.

One very important element to remember is that confrontation works best when it flows out of a context of trust, when a relationship has been established. I can handle my wife's stinging remarks because I love her and trust her and know that ultimately she tells me this because it's what's best and because she loves me, too. David could accept Nathan's judgment because they had an established relationship. Throughout the history of Israel, the king knew the prophets, and the prophets knew the king; they were interrelated. David trusted Nathan as a prophet of the Lord. It's rarely appropriate to approach someone you've never met and confront him or her. All you'll accomplish by doing so is turning someone angry without inspiring even a hint of life change.

Spurring One Another On

In Hebrews, we are reminded what our foundational motivation should be when we confront others: "Let us consider how we may spur one another on toward love and good deeds" (10:24). This metaphor was definitely not written arbitrarily. I found that out from a tall, lanky, dyed-in-the-wool Colorado cowboy I know who wears boots, a hat, and a belt buckle the size of a motorcycle license plate. We were talking one day about this idea of spurring one another on, and he told me that the reason cowboys wear spurs is to poke the horse when they desire for the horse to move in a specific direction. The spur doesn't break the skin of the horse, but it isn't comfortable, either. The spur provides enough pain and discomfort to get the animal moving quickly. Even if the horse could, it would never look up at its rider and say, "Wow, that felt good. Can you get the left side, too?"[8]

In the same way, when we get spurred on by others, it's uncomfortable, but it inspires us to run in the direction in which we are intended to run and live the life we are intended to live.[9] Confrontation is a part of our role as a community.[10] We need to be Nathans for each other: people willing to take the risk and confront even when it's easier to turn our head. And we need to be like David, who received admonishment with love and the willingness to change.

What would that look like if the church functioned like a community that spurred one another on even when it got uncomfortable? What would it look like if we took the risk of humbly confronting or being confronted? I believe it would mean a community of believers who watched out for one another and graciously brought one another back when we've strayed away. We'd be a group of people who sharpened one another to be refined followers of Christ.

The body of Christ needs you and you need the body of Christ even when it hurts.

Going Further

1. Have you ever experienced a positive confrontation situation? A negative one?

2. How do you usually react when confronted? Why?

3. When you know you should confront someone, do you go through with it, or do you shrink back?

4. Why is it easier to avoid confrontation? What are you afraid might happen if you confronted someone?

5 We normally focus on the negatives of confrontation, but what are the potential positives?

Be courageous. Even as you stand there hiding in the bushes, shaking to the bottom of your toes, frightened of what's to follow, what consequences will come of it, know that evil will not prevail. That you are not alone. That you bring the kingdom of God, and there is hope. There is hope always. And others will walk out of dark places and see you standing there, arms outstretched, given completely to this hope.

—David Crowder

You will come to a place where the streets are not marked. Some windows are lighted. But mostly they're darked. A place you could sprain both your elbow and chin! Do you dare to stay out? Do you dare to go in? How much can you lose? How much can you win?

—Dr. Seuss

8 GAMBLING ON GOD

ABRAHAM, THE FATHER OF OUR FAITH

In April 1519, Spanish conquistador Hernando Cortez and almost four hundred of his men set sail on a mission to discover new land. They arrived near Veracruz, on Mexico's eastern shore, not quite knowing what to expect. Shortly after coming ashore, Cortez ordered his crew members to do the unthinkable: burn the ships. Before they knew what they would discover in this uncharted territory, their commander forced them to eliminate their only form of transportation and unpack their bags. Cortez and his men were in Mexico to stay.[1]

That story makes me think about what it means to follow Jesus. We have no idea what territory we will discover; our future is completely unclear. Jesus said, "No one who puts his hand to the plow and looks back is fit for service in the kingdom of God" (Luke 9:62). Living for God means burning our ships. That's what this chapter is all about: following God even though we have no idea where He's going. And the risk? Well, who knows what dangers lie ahead? It'd be a lot safer to follow a path we already know. But when we take the risk to follow God's path, the future unfolds in a greater, more fulfilling adventure.

William Ernest Henley penned the famously arrogant lines "I am the master of my fate; I am the captain of my soul."[2] One evening at Pierced Chapel, the community of faith of which I am a pastor, singer/songwriter Kelly Minter discussed the topic of risk in our personal lives.[3] Referring to Henley's statement, she said we often believe that the riskiest thing we could ever do is to turn our lives over to Christ. Despite this rugged individualism that is often praised in our culture and is evident in Henley's words, Kelly proposed that living the way Henley suggests is the riskiest thing we could ever do. It leaves us in a position to risk everything, including our eternal futures. Determining to be the master of our own fate and the captain of our own soul leaves us in a dangerously vulnerable spot. It is only Jesus who deserves to be in the role of master and captain. That's why Jesus said, "What good will it be for a man if he gains the whole world, yet forfeits his soul? Or what can a man give in exchange for his soul?" (Matthew 16:26).

The English word *risk* comes from the Greek word *paraboluothai*, a term that describes gambling. Its literal meaning is, "To stake everything on the turn of the dice."[4] Where our futures are concerned, we can gamble at two different tables. We can be the master of our fate, taking the safe road, risking an empty life, or we can sit at God's table and gamble on the hope that He's got the best future in mind for us, but knowing that we may stumble or be knocked over along the way.

There is a passage in the Old Testament that tells of a gambler who risked his whole future by trusting God. Abraham—a man familiar to millions of people and claimed as the founding father of Christianity, Islam, and Judaism—demonstrates one of the biggest gambles on God of all time. In the twenty-second chapter of Genesis, we read the story referred to in Christianity as "the sacrifice of Isaac," where God tested Abraham's faith by asking him to sacrifice his son. In a sense, this phrase—"the sacrifice of Isaac"—is a bit of a misnomer, because Abraham never completely sacrificed his son. The Jews, however, call this passage the *Akedah*, a Hebrew word that means "the binding of Isaac." And the story in the Muslim faith is referred to as the *dhabih*, which comes from the Arabic verb meaning "to cut, rend, or slit."[5] All three names for this passage accurately imply the depth of the story. In all three religions, this story represents the epitome of living in complete trust of God. It is the central story of the life of Abraham and is quite confusing, perplexing, and even disturbing.

The story begins with God calling out Abraham's name and saying to him, "Take your son, your only son, Isaac, whom you love, and go to the region of Moriah. Sacrifice him there as a burnt offering on one of the mountains I will tell you about" (Genesis 22:2).

What?

It seems a bit cruel of God, doesn't it, to tell Abraham to not only kill his son, Isaac, but to take *his only son*, Isaac? *His only son whom he loves?* Talk about hammering the hurt deeper.[6]

In fact, God points out that Isaac is Abraham's only son *four times*. Clearly, God is trying to emphasize that this sacrifice will not be small or easy. In fact, it will without question be the most difficult thing Abraham's ever had to do.

God's End of the Bargain

In order for us to understand the true depth of God's request of Abraham, we have to step back a little bit. Earlier in Abraham's life (before Isaac was even born), God promised Abraham that he would be the father of many nations (see Genesis 12:2-3). It was quite a promise to a wandering nomad from the desert. It may seem too obvious for me to even say, but in order to be the father of many nations, you need to start with having a lot of children—or, at the very least, *one*.

God makes the promise to Abraham, who then retorts, "But God, why don't I have any children then?" (see Genesis 15:2-3). Abraham isn't complaining or being disrespectful to God. He believes God but definitely doesn't understand what He's doing. Abraham had what is called in Hebrew *chutzpah*. It is not faith; it is much stronger than that. *Chutzpah* is an intense, never-say-die, unwavering, stubborn commitment to God.[7] It is a willingness to trust in such a way that reaches beyond common sense. One with *chutzpah* trusts even when what God says seems completely contradictory to who God is.

Not only did Abraham and his wife, Sarah, not have any children, they also were really old. Sarah, at the age of eighty-nine, was well past her window of opportunity for getting pregnant, so when three men visited their tent and told her that at this time next year she would have a son, Sarah laughed.[8] This was a difficult piece of news to believe at their age, you know. But Sarah's laughter didn't stop God from swooping down into human history and allowing Sarah to become pregnant. She gave birth to a son, Isaac, which happens to mean "laughter." It was now looking as though God's promise that Abraham was to father many nations, as crazy as it sounded earlier, might come to fruition.

Needless to say, when God asked Abraham to sacrifice his son, Abraham was confused. Again, how was he to father many nations without an heir? If Isaac died, would God impregnate Sarah *again*? Did God mean "father of many nations" figuratively? Was God being cruel? What was going on?

When God asked Abraham for Isaac, He was asking Abraham to risk his future and the future of many generations that would come after him. God asked him to risk what he knew, what made sense, in order to trust His sovereign plan.

Abraham's End of the Bargain

Abraham and Sarah lived in the southern city of Beersheva, believed to have been at the southern tip of Israel.[9] From Beersheva, God told Abraham to take a three-day journey to the region of Moriah. It is generally accepted that Moriah refers to Mount Moriah, one of the highest points and most significant pieces of property for the Jews in the world.[10] (It's a significant piece of property for Muslims as well. Muslims believe that it was on the peak of this mountain that Mohammed received his revelation and then made his nocturnal flight to Mecca.) For Jews and Christians, it was on this exact location in Jerusalem where Solomon's temple was constructed—where God's presence dwelt among God's people. Jesus made many visits to the temple on Mount Moriah. As you have probably picked up on by now, the significance is thick: This story of Abraham occurs in the exact location as the building where God's presence resided among His chosen people. God was using this location as a way of reminding the people that God is in control of human history and will keep His promises to sustain the chosen people of God.[11]

Genesis 22:3 tells us that early in the morning, Abraham collected his things, loaded up his donkey, and took Isaac and two servants with him on a three-day journey to the region of Moriah. I find it interesting that the text never records Abraham mentioning any of this to Sarah. Maybe Abraham didn't have the guts to tell her where they were going. I doubt he told the two servants, either. The text also never records that he told Isaac where they were going or what they were doing or why. But we do know that Isaac carried the wood on his own back.[12]

On the journey, Isaac, being the insightful son that he was, asked his father where the sacrifice was. The wood, the knife, and the fire were present, but where was the object of sacrifice? (verse 7). What a taxing question that must have been for Abraham to hear from his son. This trip would go down as one of the most memorable father-son outings in the history of mankind.

In our Christian tradition, we tend to envision Isaac as a young child or a teenager, yet many Jewish scholars believe that Isaac was a grown man, possibly as old as thirty. Some Jewish scholars believe Isaac could have been as old as thirty-seven. It's much easier to imagine a child, one who couldn't defend himself or who was naive. But the story is much more rich when we understand that Isaac was probably old enough to fight for his life but didn't.

Can you imagine the horror Isaac must have felt when he realized that *he* was the sacrifice? And what about Abraham? Imagine the absolute torment he must have felt while raising a knife to his only son, whom he loved.[13]

128 Here I Am

As Abraham raised the knife, an angel of the Lord called out to him twice. Abraham responded exactly the same as he responded at the beginning of the story: "Here I am!" (Genesis 22:11). Abraham wasn't stating his geographic location; instead, he was announcing his willingness to do what God said. He was reporting for duty.[14] I wonder if Abraham then dreaded the possibilities of what might be said to him. What would God ask of him this time?

The instruction, he learned quickly, was to stop and not do anything to his son.

The Lord said, "Now I know that you fear God, because you have not withheld from me your son, your only son" (verse 12). Then Abraham looked up and saw a ram whose horns were stuck in the brush. He took the ram and sacrificed it in place of his son. After Abraham sacrificed the ram, God reiterated His promise:

"I swear by myself . . . that because you have done this and have not withheld your son, your only son, I will surely bless you and make your descendants as numerous as the stars in the sky and as the sand on the seashore. Your descendents will take possession of the cities of their enemies, and through your offspring all nations on earth will be blessed, because you have obeyed me" (verses 15-18).

Abraham had gambled on God with his future. He had every reason to doubt that God would fulfill His end of the promise, but Abraham took Him at His word. Although there was much more at stake than the future of himself and Isaac, he risked for the future of thousands of generations after him. And he had passed the test—one of the most difficult tests ever presented to a father, or to a human being for that matter. Abraham returned to his servants and left Moriah (verse 19). (Interestingly, the text does not mention Isaac after this. Might Isaac have run away in fear?)

Maybe you feel as though you have every reason to doubt that God wants the best for your life or that He will keep His end of the bargain or that He will come through in the end. But what if you believed that God will actually do what He says He will do? God has made clear that He wants to give you a hopeful future and desires that you live life to the absolute fullest measure. Will you trust Him with your future?

We never are told that trusting God with our future will be easy. In fact, it might completely ruin everything you have going for you. But think about how it can make possible what *God* has going for you.

Sacrifice

So, is Abraham's example of trust-at-all-cost mentality just some obscure example to be admired, but not followed? Not at all.

Abraham's story demonstrates to all of us that God's promises can be trusted. Our obedience to Him can change the course of history, although we may never know it. And although you may not hear a booming voice from an angel as Abraham did, you can still hear God's voice. Maybe distinguishing God's call means paying attention to the opportunities in front of you. Maybe there's a fork in the road. On one side, there's a safe path that leads you to the life you know, like living at your parents' house instead of taking that fantastic job offer across the country, or marrying your boyfriend because you're comfortable, but not in love, with him. On the other side, the road is dangerous because it leads to that job across the country or a life without your boyfriend.

Or maybe paying attention to God's call means being sensitive to His Word and His Spirit. We know that His Spirit guides us[15] and that His Word influences us.[16] Jeremiah tells us God has a plan for us; it's our job to ask and to listen for what that plan may be.

130

You may remember the media attention a few years ago concerning Pat Tillman. He seemed to have a lot going for him. After a great college football career as a linebacker at Arizona State University, he was drafted by the Arizona Cardinals to play professional football. After four years of playing in the NFL, he decided to make a dramatic change. In the wake of the 9/11 terrorist attacks, Pat turned down a three-year, $3.6 million contract extension from the Cardinals to enlist in the army for only $18,000 a year as a Ranger. "My great-grandfather was at Pearl Harbor, and a lot of my family has . . . gone and fought in wars, and I really haven't done a . . . thing as far as laying myself on the line like that," Tillman told NBC News after the terrorist attacks on the World Trade Center.[17] Although people respected his altruistic intentions, many thought he was crazy for turning down the life of fame and fortune most people only dream of. In May of 2002, he quit playing professional football and along with his brother Kevin, enlisted in the army. After fighting in Iraq, he was eventually shipped to Afghanistan with Kevin, fighting on the front lines. He was killed in battle on April 22, 2004, at age twenty-seven.

Michael Bidwill, vice president of the Cardinals, said, "He was a brave man. There are very few people who have the courage to do what he did, the courage to walk away from a professional sports career and make the ultimate sacrifice."[18] Pat was sure that risking his established future plans, the life so many long for, in exchange for contributing to a greater good, a higher calling, was worth it. He risked the uncertainty of his future so that our freedom in America could be preserved.[19] The Arizona Cardinals, the National Football League, and millions around the world have paid tribute to this modern-day hero. I find it a bit ironic that although he played the safety position on the football field, in life, he gravitated toward what was risky and worthy, not what was safe. Pat gave his life to a cause much nobler than a mere game, and because of it, he's now considered a hero.

Just imagine if you and I were willing to risk our future and lay down our safety in order to live for the higher cause of Christ, something that would outlast even the most worthy of causes here on this earth. When you gave your life to Jesus Christ, you risked your entire future for the purpose of His glory. In a sense, it is committing suicide. You kill your own desires and yearnings and plans. Jesus' call to risk it all was a costly one: "If anyone would come after me, he must deny himself and take up his cross and follow me. For whoever wants to save his life will lose it, but whoever loses his life for me will find it" (Matthew 16:24-25).

He tells us to voluntarily pick up our own wood, the wood we will carry up the mountain to sacrifice our own personal plans and desires and yearnings and future—just like what happened to Jesus and almost to Isaac. When we look at the words of Jesus through the context of Abraham's story, it seems almost morbid and gruesome and extremely difficult.

And it *is* morbid and gruesome and extremely difficult. That's why making a lifelong commitment to Jesus Christ comes at a greater cost than just simply bowing our heads and repeating a prayer. That's the start of the process, but it does not even compare to following closely and passionately on Jesus' heels. The call to pick up our crosses is one of the greatest twists of divine paradox ever spoken, because while we die, we truly live. And it creates a lot more question marks than exclamation points. Oswald Chambers once wrote, "Certainty is the mark of the common-sense life; gracious uncertainty is the mark of the spiritual life. To be certain of God means that we are uncertain in all our ways. . . . This is generally said with a sigh of sadness; it should rather be an expression of breathless expectation."[20]

What if instead of dreading uncertainty we embraced it with enthusiasm? What if we saw following God as part of the adventure, part of life lived to the fullest, rather than a waiting game we tolerate and hope is over soon? Letting go of our future and placing it in God's lap means not knowing the ending, but isn't that better? When we know the ending, it takes away all of the fun.

Maybe the secret to the risk-filled life rests in this shift of our thinking. Maybe if we could embrace rather than run from the unknown, we could experience a revolutionized relationship with Jesus and a transformed way to approaching our everyday lives.

The story of Abraham and his risky obedience is one of the most sobering challenges we could ever accept in our relationship with God. Living like Abraham means risking our careers, our five-year plans, our desires and yearnings and passions, our relationships, our security, and our well-being.

Plain and simple, Jesus says, following Him will cost you *everything*. What He wants is for us to set our ships on fire and trust that He will take care of us.

Going Further

1. The original meaning of the word *risk* is "to gamble." What does it mean for you to gamble on God?

2. Would those who know you describe you as "a gambler for God"? Why or why not? Do you want to be described that way? What would it take for others to describe you in that way?

3. How does the story of Abraham make you see God?

4. What does risking your future look like?

5. Does a lack of certainty excite you or paralyze you?

He is no fool who gives what he cannot
keep to gain what he cannot lose.

—Jim Elliot

Many would be cowards if they had the
courage enough.

—Thomas Fuller

What our age lacks is not reflection, but
passion.

—Søren Kierkegaard

If God is for us, who can be against us?

—the apostle Paul

WHEN GOD SAYS JUMP

A BENEDICTION

n high school my friend Tyler invited me to go with him to a place called The Quarry. On our thirty-minute drive there, Tyler explained that over the past thirty years, the old, abandoned, secret limestone pit had filled with water—up to eighty feet in some places—and was perfect for cliff jumping. As he described this place, I acted nonchalant, but I was so freaked out that I felt as if my throat would close up.

Tyler parked the car, and we wandered through the woods until we reached an opening in the trees. Far below us was a massive bowl that looked bigger than a football field.

"Follow me," he said as he whipped off his shirt and approached the ledge of doom. "It's not as scary as you think." (He must have sensed my fear.)

I looked over the edge. *Yeah right. Are you kidding me?*

I got dizzy and almost pooped my pants. I'm not scared of heights, but the thought of free-falling into an unfamiliar bowl of water was a totally new concept for me. *How was I to get out? What if I hit something? What if something bit me?* This was not a jump off the city pool's diving board. I was playing with the big boys now.

Tyler went first, without any apparent hesitation or anxiety. He took a few steps back, bounded forward, let out a rebel yell, placed his arms above his head like a pencil, and plunged into the water. As he returned to the surface, he laughed freely and motioned for me to join him in the abyss below. Standing with my toes on the ledge and looking down at Tyler, who from where I stood looked like an ant, I thought of how foolish this whole summer afternoon activity seemed and wondered why I agreed to join him in the first place.

"You can't think about it. Just jump!" he shouted.

138   "Shut up. Don't rush me."

After a few moments of mind games with myself, I leaned forward and jumped. Screaming, partly out of thrill but mostly out of sheer terror, I hit the water and sank to depths I'm not sure I'd been before. After reaching the surface and wiping water from my eyes, I heard Tyler clapping.

"So, what'd you think?" he yelled out.

"Let's do it again!" Completely exhilarated, we swam to shore together, climbed the long trail back to the top, and jumped again and again. We must have jumped into The Quarry at least two dozen times. Looking back, I can't imagine *not* doing it—it was so worth the risk.

There certainly is a thrill to the adventure of taking risks. It's a thrill that can be so rewarding it's almost addictive, a thrill that makes you proudly stick out your chest and want to shout, "I did it!"

Sure, my jump into the quarry wasn't a significantly life-changing event, but the courage that I mustered up that afternoon definitely spread into other areas of my life, showing me in a real, tangible way that while it was terrifying, it was thrilling. It was worth it.

The characters of Scripture we've studied—Joseph and Jeremiah and Philip and Mary—experienced either moments of sheer terror or moments of what-the-heck-am-I-thinking second guesses. But I believe that each one of them would have been able to look back and say they would like to do it again.

The list of biblical risk takers we've explored in the pages of this book is far from exhaustive. In fact, it's just a hint at what's inside Scripture. The Old and New Testaments are filled with people who had normal lives—normal, that is, until the one day they deliberately chose to step off the ledge and jump, turning their whole worlds upside down. The warrior Gideon, the stuttering Moses, the young Gentile woman Ruth, the younger brother Joseph, the prophet Elijah, the rich man Joseph of Arimathea, the prostitute Rahab, the first martyr Stephen, the gospel writer Matthew. Many, if not most, of these men and women never would have been on the cover of any national magazine during their lifetime. In fact, most of them were far from the typical risk taker: Abraham was a wanderer, Moses was a murderer, Ruth was a widowed foreigner, Elijah was suicidal, Matthew was in a despised vocation, nobody cared about Jeremiah, Shadrach and his two buddies were teenagers, and you certainly wouldn't want to bring Rahab home to your mother. Despite their sketchy pasts and the multiple strikes against them, they chose to take the leap of faith. Their lifestyles radically changed, and their influence increased exponentially. They risked big for the kingdom of God and were given life like never before. God said jump, and they obeyed.[1]

I am encouraged when I read about these "nobodies." (Obviously, someone thought they were important because their stories ended up in the Word of God.) I have often felt that my circle of influence isn't big enough or that my position isn't as influential as, say, a congressman on Capitol Hill or an actor in Hollywood. But these stories help me remember that God's the one who is powerful enough and knowledgeable enough to have placed you and me here in the first place. And if God is this big and powerful and knowledgeable, then He surely knows how to influence His kingdom through me. Regardless, I'm called to be faithful whether I'm a congressman or an actor or a pastor or a barista or a student or a telemarketer.

The Passion in Risk

I've learned that risk induces passion like nothing else can. For example, after my jump into The Quarry, I became full of life, ready to keep jumping. Or after deciding to marry my wife, I felt a love for her like I've never felt for anyone else. Passion is a funny thing because it'll drive a person to behave in ways that just don't make sense at all. The late Mike Yaconelli was one of those passionate people who lived in a way that honored Jesus and confused people. In his book *Dangerous Wonder*, Mike wrote, "Passion is always risky. The Bible gives example after example of people who fell in love with Jesus and left their jobs, their families, their security. Once people met Jesus, their passion became hazardous to their health. . . . Passion is not something to be treated lightly. The passionate life is a risky life. The question is: Is the passionate life worth the risk?"[2] In short, passionate people are risk takers for God's kingdom.

When I meet people for the first time, I often ask them what their passions are. Sometimes I get a blank stare. But then I follow up with, "What is that one area of your life that's so important that you would risk doing something big for it even if you might fail?" Usually I get a thoughtful answer that in some way reveals what those individuals are proud of, what they value, what they are passionate about.

Those great men and women of the faith all throughout Scripture were passionate people. They were passionate about their God and making His name known in their circle of influence. I would venture to say that being aware of one's passions sparks the opportunity and desire for risk. I also believe that being aware of risks we are willing (or unwilling) to make reveals a lot about what we are passionate about (or what we are not). All of the passionate people I know are constantly taking risks. Conversely, sometimes I interact with people who have admitted to me that they are just downright bored with life. These are the most predictable, safe, protected, risk-phobic people I know. Needless to say, their lives are not contagious, and I don't think this is a coincidence, either.

I think it's important to understand that risks are hard, but when we're just so dang passionate about something, it almost doesn't **141** matter. If your house were burning down and you got out safely but remembered that your infant son was still in the house asleep, you would run back into the house without much thought about it, no matter how dangerous it may seem. Our risks fall in line with our passions. They reveal what is important to us. Wouldn't you agree?

> Jeremiah was more passionate about serving God than he was about succeeding.
>
> Philip was more passionate about listening to the prompting of the Holy Spirit than he was about the revival of Samaria.
>
> Joseph was more passionate about protecting his fiancée and obeying the angel than he was about his reputation.
>
> The three teenage guys were more passionate about the truth of the King than about the lies of a king.

And on and on and on.

Difficult but Worth It

Whether we succeed or not when we take risks, we usually discover two important realities (sometimes without even knowing it):

1. Risk is hard.

2. Risk is worth it.

Sometimes risk is a heart-pumping adrenaline rush, but often risk is backbreaking work that doesn't always equate to fun. I'm sure Shadrach, Meshach, and Abednego didn't think the furnace was a blast (no pun intended). I'm certain Jeremiah didn't dream of being locked in the stocks for a while among his townspeople. Nor was Joseph excited about facing his friends and family when he decided to stick by Mary's side and believe her wild story of how she got pregnant. But ultimately in each situation, these individuals would admit to us that *it was worth the effort.* That's why the Bible tells us, "All these people were still living by faith when they died. . . . People who say such things show that they are looking for a country of their own. If they had been thinking of the country they had left, they would have the opportunity to return. Instead, they were long-ing for a better country—a heavenly one" (Hebrews 11:13-16). Paraphrasing here, "They had kingdom passions, not earthly ones. Passions that didn't just serve their own interests, but instead served to impact the kingdom of God."

I think if we are going to participate in taking risks, we have to be convinced the risks are worth the effort. The more we're convinced of risk's value in our lives, the more we're willing to jump.

Taking The Risk

If we're honest with ourselves, we'd all admit we've wondered if the risk of following Jesus is worth it. And that's understandable, because following Jesus is not a risk—it is *The* Risk. It is the most significant, freakiest, meaningful, costly risk we could ever take. And I don't mean just the risk of saying a prayer and waiting until we die.

It's like the line made famous in *Braveheart*, "All men die. Few men ever really live." Risking our lives for Jesus can rescue us from a boring, mundane life that holds no meaning or purpose or adventure. Jesus inspires us to risk so that we may really live (see John 10:10).

Rewards

For the most part, I think we fail to see the entire picture of why we should participate in risky living for the kingdom of God. We dwell on what we might lose in the midst of risk and fail to grasp the rewards God has promised that we can gain. The word *reward* makes some Christians nervous. *We aren't supposed to focus on rewards,* they think. *That sounds so selfish.* But Scripture makes it clear that the Christian life includes rewards. There are seventy-five references in your Bible to the concept of rewards, many spoken by Jesus Himself.[3]

143

The author of Hebrews writes this about rewards: "Without faith it is impossible to please God, because anyone who comes to him must believe that he exists and that *he rewards those who earnestly seek him*" (Hebrews 11:6, emphasis added). So, we are assured there are rewards, but what *are* the rewards—both here on this earth and in eternity—when we take risks? Well, there are earthly rewards, which include respect from others and opportunities to influence others. But then there are heavenly rewards (which also play a part in our earthly lives), including the unbelievable privilege of participating in real and abundant life that Jesus offers.

A life of adventure and passion and purpose and risk is extremely rewarding. But I admit, I searched the Word for specific rewards, and they're just not there. And to be honest, it was a bit frustrating. If there are incentives to following Jesus—rewards—then why didn't Jesus list them in bullet points so we knew what we might be gaining? Or why didn't God add an appendix to the Ten Commandments to show the Israelites the benefits of obedience? Why wouldn't He make the eternal incentives of risk-filled living more appealing and inviting and obvious? We want all the answers, and He just isn't supplying them. But this, quite possibly, could be a good thing.

If all God did was list the incentives for taking risks, then maybe we would treat our relationship with Him like a job, where we work certain hours a day to collect a paycheck. We would risk something just to receive the goods. But that would make us nothing more than spiritual consumers. If people claim risk-filled living has nothing to do with rewards, they'd be flat-out unbiblical. But on the other hand, if others claim we risk *because* of its rewards, they, too, would be wrong, for our primary incentive is God and God alone.

144

The apostle Paul used a sports metaphor to explain our purpose in life. He wrote, "Run in such a way as to get the prize" (1 Corinthians 9:24).[4] The prize of Paul's day was a garland of laurel leaves that would be placed on the head of victorious athletes. But did athletes really spend months—even years—of their lives training to receive a goofy-looking crown of leaves that would dry out and wither in less than a week? Of course not. The crown acted as only a tangible representation of the joy of competing, completing, and succeeding in the games to the best of their ability.

One of the U.S. Olympic Training Centers is located in our city of Colorado Springs. A handful of the athletes who trained for the 2004 Summer Olympic Games in Athens attended a Bible study I led every Tuesday night in the months leading up to the games. Those attending the Bible study were training in wrestling, tae kwon do, archery, men's and women's volleyball, and men's and women's weight lifting. Tara Nott-Cunningham attended the study on occasion. Tara had won a gold medal in weight lifting in the 2000 Summer Olympics in Sydney and was hoping to defend her gold medal in Athens. I asked her if all of this physical torture of her body and the long days of training were worth it for her medal. Her response was interesting.

It wasn't for the medal, she said. It was for the joy of knowing that after all these years of training—the injuries and sore muscles and late nights and strict diet—she had competed and completed and succeeded. And that was enough for her. That's why, she said, so many athletes cry on the medal stand when the medal is placed around their neck and the National Anthem is played. The joy runs too deep and it hits that this moment is an emotional culmination of all the excruciating moments before it.

I believe that one day when we are in heaven—after a lifetime of gut-wrenching, scary, intense, risk-filled days—we'll stand on a medal stand and God will place crowns upon our heads. And we will stand there with tears streaming down our cheeks, knowing that we've done it: We competed, we completed, and we succeeded in this life as it was meant to be lived.   **145**

Above all else, I am convinced we will grasp the fact that the incentive of risk is God Himself. The rewards are not more stuff but an intimate, pleasing, loving, close relationship with a God who is pleased with us and looks at us and says, "You did it!"

God Is Enough

My hope for you is that you are encouraged by these ordinary men and women of the faith who were more passionate about God than they were about their reputations or wallets or futures. They reached the end of their earthly lives pleased with their faith and the risks they took for the kingdom of God. And they could see the smile on God's face as He expressed His pleasure as well.

A life of risk will be intimidating/demanding/difficult/lonely/ overwhelming/troublesome/uncomfortable. But serving God is worth the risk, because God is enough. It's better for us to risk something for which we are passionate about and fail than to never risk at all, because more important than safety is the pleasure of God.

I love to write in journals, so I have lots of them stacked in our basement. Every now and then, I go downstairs, find my old box of journals, and read what I wrote in years past. In the process of writing this book, I came across a prayer I had scribbled in my journal several years back about this idea of living courageously for God:

> God, make me a man of courage—courage to love my wife, to not care what people think of me, to do what people said I could never do, to make history, to make Christ known, to conquer adventures. Give me courage to live deeply, laugh loudly, care genuinely, pray passionately, and live richly. Give me courage to follow desires, attempt big things (and fail at some of them), live boldly, love graciously, forgive freely, and look back on my life and possess no regrets. What would the world look like if it were filled with courageous men and women instead of timid, bored, dutiful, apathetic, and secure individuals? How different would we be living out Christ's mission on earth if we were passionately filled with courage? And what if it started with me? What would it look like to be known as a man who was wild, dangerous, not afraid of anything or anyone? God, this is how I want to live my life for You.

Survey Says...

Just recently I read about a fascinating study in which researchers interviewed men and women who were ninety-five years old or older. The researchers asked the respondents just this one question:

If you had to do life all over again, what would you do differently? There were various answers to this question—some serious, some silly—but most of them landed in one of three main categories: they would reflect more, they would do or create something that would last after they were dead, and they would take more risks. They would live life with more adventure, take more chances, reach for things that seemed impossible or ridiculous. Life would carry more meaning and significance.

I find great wisdom as well as a challenge in the words of our elders. I don't know about you, but when I'm ninety-five, I don't want to look back at my life and say I wished I had taken more risks. (Why live with haunting regrets in the final chapter of my life on top of losing my hearing, eyesight, and, maybe by that point, marbles?)

You can risk it. I believe you can. Others need you. The world needs you. And God is looking for people to stand up and risk for His glory. Risk for the kingdom of God. There is too much at stake for you not to.

Just a few days before I graduated from college, a friend wrote a letter of congratulations. In that letter, he included a prayer by Sir Francis Drake. Even today, I have this prayer tacked to the wall in my office, and now I can think of no greater way to end this book than to share it with you:[5]

> Disturb us, Lord,
>> when we are too well pleased with ourselves;
>> when our dreams have come true because we dreamed too little;
>> when we arrive safely because we sailed too close to the shore.
> Disturb us, Lord, when with the abundance of things we possess
>> we have lost our thirst for the waters of life; having fallen in love
>> with life, we have ceased to dream of eternity;
>> and in our efforts to build a new earth,
>> we have allowed our vision of the new heaven to dim.

Disturb us, Lord, to dare more boldly,
    to venture on wider seas where storms will show Your mastery;
    where losing sight of land, we shall find the stars.
We ask You to push back the horizons of our hopes,
    and to push us into the future in strength, courage, hope and love.

148

Notes

Introduction

1. Reggie McNeal (lecture, The Present-Future Church Conference, Phantom Canyon Brewery, Colorado Springs, CO, April 18, 2005).

2. John Eldredge, *Wild at Heart Field Manual: A Personal Guide to Discover the Secret of Your Masculine Soul* (Nashville: Nelson, 2002), 254.

3. Bruce Tremper, quoted in John Fry, "The Arrogance of Risk," *SKI Magazine* (January 2005), 65–66.

4. Tremper, 65–66.

5. Maybe I just know a lot of boring people.

6. Philip Yancey, *The Jesus I Never Knew* (Grand Rapids, MI: Zondervan, 1995), 14–15.

7. Dorothy Sayers, "The Greatest Drama Ever Staged," *The Whimsical Christian* (New York: Collier Books, 1978), 14.

8. Michael Yaconelli, *Dangerous Wonder: The Adventure of Childlike Faith* (Colorado Springs, CO: NavPress, 2003), 40.

Chapter 1 — Rebelling for a Good Cause

1. It made me a bit queasy to see the former president's bloodstains on the chair fabric where his head was resting when he was shot.

2. For examples, see Exodus 23:19; Leviticus 7:23-24; 13:47-52.

3. The book of Acts is a great book to teach us what it means to influence the world.

4. God has a keen interest in using teenagers for some reason. Scholars believe that Jesus' mother, Mary, was a teenager when Jesus was born, in addition to the shepherds who visited the Christ child. Scholars believe that all the twelve disciples of Jesus were in their teenage years as well.

5. The ruins of Babylon can be found in modern-day Iraq.

6. John H. Walton, Victor H. Matthews, and Mark W. Chavalas, *The IVP Bible Background Commentary: Old Testament* (Downers Grove, IL: InterVarsity, 2000), 734.

7. One time I was teaching on this story, and I accidentally said *prostate.* Needless to say, I was embarrassed.

8. The CDs burned rather quickly as a result.

9. Women, mothers especially, have this superhuman power to smell any odor not considered normal.

10. Eugene H. Peterson, introduction to the book of Daniel, *The Message* (Colorado Springs, CO: NavPress, 2002), 1579.

Chapter 2—Dumping $50K on a Pair of Dirty Feet

1. Read the account of Jesus raising Lazarus from the dead in John 11.

2. Knowing this adds significance when the Gospels record Jesus inviting Himself over to the house of Zacchaeus, and Pharisees grumbling when Jesus accepted invitations to eat meals at the home of "sinners." It would have meant He accepted the "sinners" for who they were. No Jewish rabbi would have accepted those invitations.

3. In *Where Is God When It Hurts?* (Grand Rapids, MI: Zondervan, 2002), Philip Yancey and Dr. Paul Brand go into great detail about the effects of leprosy on the human body. They write that pain is actually a gift of God.

4. My friend Josh told me he used to make fun of his classmates in sixth grade by calling them "nard." But this was before he knew that it meant "perfume."

5. Craig S. Keener, *The IVP Bible Background Commentary: New Testament* (Downers Grove, IL: InterVarsity, 1993), 294.

6. Some of you are probably thinking, *If that's the case, I probably should get another job.*

7. She also could have been rebuked for her risqué foot cleaning with her hair.

8. Mike Yankoski, *Under the Overpass: A Journey of Faith on the Streets of America* (Sisters, OR: Multnomah, 2005), 15.

9. Yankoski, 15.

10. They left whatever money they had in the bank and committed to not touching even a cent of it while doing this experiment— no cutting corners allowed.

11. Yankoski, 22.

12. Jim Collins, *Good to Great: Why Some Companies Make the Leap . . . And Others Don't* (New York: HarperCollins, 2001), 1.

13. You'd probably invite Jesus to your house, too, if He had raised your brother from the dead.

14. "Galileo," http://library.thinkquest.org/J0112388/galileo.htm.

Chapter 3 — Ruining Your Reputation

1. This age difference kind of reminds me of Tom Cruise and Katie Holmes.

2. Notice how the text refers to Joseph as Mary's husband although they were not yet married.

3. Other translations (for example, NLT and NKJV) use the word *just* instead of *righteous*. And *The Message* says it colorfully: "Joseph, chagrined but noble, determined to take care of things quietly."

4. Concerning this discussion on stoning an adulterer, see John 8:1-11 for the story of Jesus and the woman caught in adultery.

5. Consider the similarities of the Pharisees' fears to the response Adam gave after he sinned in the Garden of Eden. In Genesis 3:10, Adam responded to God with, "I heard you in the garden, and I was afraid because I was naked; so I hid." Adam was exposed and tried to hide it.

6. Leo Horrigan, www.zmag.org/quotes/.

7. Don't ask me how I got the job—it's a long story. I guess you could say I stumbled onto the gig.

Chapter 4 — Investing in the Messy

1. While the story is completely accurate, Eddie is not the real name of the salesman at the time-share company. I really wanted to list Eddie's real name, but better judgment told me I shouldn't. If I did, he just might come and knock on my front door and try to sell me something again, and I don't want that.

2. For transportation, most people walked; some were wealthy enough to ride a donkey, but only the most elite rode in chariots. There is a great possibility the chariot was actually moving, which might be why he ran up to it.

3. "Wales Rugby Fan Loses His Tackle," http://www.inthenews.co.uk/ quirky/body-and-appearance/health/wales-rugby-fan-loses -his-tackle-$7755396.htm.

4. Jesus told a wonderful parable about what it means to get involved as Philip did. It's the parable of the Good Samaritan found in Luke 10:25-37. As you read it, notice the excuse of inconvenience and unavailability of the religious leaders and their unwillingness to get involved in a physically, financially, or spiritually messy situation.

Chapter 5—Having a No-Good, Very Bad Day   153

1. Bill Breen, "The Thrill of Defeat," *Fast Company*, June 2004, 76.

2. Wikipedia, "Ted Williams," http://en.wikipedia.org/wiki/Ted _Williams.

3. You'd probably want to leave that information off of a resume when applying for another job.

4. Breen, 77.

5. Eugene H. Peterson, introduction to the book of Jeremiah, *The Message* (Colorado Springs, CO: NavPress, 2002), 1342.

6. Also see Jeremiah 15:18.

7. http://www.ocytoronto.org/reflections_fernando.html.

8. He also brought success to biblical characters such as Solomon, Job, and Paul.

Chapter 6—Letting Go of Your Peanuts

1. Rob Bell, "Salvation of Our Stuff: Part 1" (Mars Hill Bible Church, Grand Rapids, MI, January 9, 2005).

2. Many people have interpreted this statement to be literal. Archaeologists have discovered there was a small and narrow gate around the walls of Jerusalem that required camels to slowly and awkwardly kneel to move through it. However, this wall was built in the Middle Ages, long after Jesus' time on earth. Therefore, when Jesus said this in the first century, there was no such gate and the statement was indeed a hyperbole, not a literal statement. See Craig S. Keener, *The IVP Bible Background Commentary* (Downers Grove, IL: InterVarsity, 1993), 240.

3. Generous Giving's official website, "What Is Generous Giving?" http://www.generousgiving.org/page.asp?sec=1&page=.

4. Bill Hybels (lecture, Willow Creek Community Church, South Barrington, IL, October, 2003).

5. My father-in-law jokingly commented that the monkeys died not from the fall but from the sudden stop.

Chapter 7—Speaking Up When You Want to Shut Up

1. See, for example, Colossians 3:16.

2. As you know, contraceptives hadn't quite made it to the shelves of the local pharmacies yet.

3. Ironically, Uriah is listed as one of David's "mighty men" (2 Samuel 23:8) in 2 Samuel 23:39, as is Bathsheba's father, Eliam, in 2 Samuel 23:34.

4. Despite all of this, God calls David a man after His own heart. It's interesting (and confusing at the same time) that some of the heroes of the faith were either murderers (Moses, David) or almost committed murder (Abraham).

5. John H. Walton, *The IVP Bible Background Commentary: Old Testament* (Downers Grove, IL: InterVarsity, 2000), 339.

6. Again, this is not to make light of the fact that the Holy Spirit does communicate with us and instructs us in our decision making. This is to show that at times, people can use the Holy Spirit's role as a cop-out for disclosing the real reason they do this or that in times of decision.

7. Chuck Colson, founder and president of Prison Fellowship, said this thought-provoking statement to a group of Christians: "I pray that you be controversial, because when you are controversial the world will begin to take notice. And when they take notice, the world will begin to see the light that is within you." (Taylor University Chapel Service, Upland, IN, Fall, 1998).

8. In addition to the metaphor of spurs, Scripture uses the metaphor of metalworking. Proverbs 27:17 says, "As iron sharpens iron, so one man sharpens another."

9. See Hebrews 3:13 and 1 Corinthians 12:12-26 for further insight.

10. For further exploration of our roles and responsibilities with other Christians, do a study on the "one another" passages in Scripture.

Chapter 8—Gambling on God

1. "Hernando Cortez," http://library.thinkquest.org/J002678F/cortez.htm.

2. William Ernest Henley, "Invictus," http://www.bartleby.com/103/7.html.

3. Kelly Minter (lecture, Pierced Chapel, Colorado Springs, CO, August 2004).

4. Lars B. Dunberg, *Becoming a Risk-Taker for God* (Colorado Springs, CO: Global Action, 2003), 26.

5. Bruce Feiler, *Abraham: A Journey to the Heart of Three Faiths* (New York: HarperCollins, 2002), 103.

6. Christian existentialist Søren Kierkegaard explored many of these difficult questions in his compelling book *Fear and Trembling*, which studies the story of Abraham and Isaac in depth.

7. Ray Vander Laan (lecture, Willow Creek Community Church, South Barrington, IL, August 1, 2002).

8. Read about this fascinating account in Genesis 18.

9. The phrase "from Dan to Beersheva" is used throughout the Old Testament to express the entirety of Israel, implying from the northern tip (Dan) to the southern tip (Beersheva). It would parallel the phrase "from New York to Los Angeles."

10. Some scholars believe there was another location called Moriah, a distance of three days' journey from Beersheva.

11. As you study Scripture, notice the significance of location. The location of many biblical stories is almost as important as the plot itself.

12. Notice the foreshadowing of a Father making His Son, His only Son, carry the wood on which He would soon die. Sound familiar? See Matthew 3:17; John 19:17-18; John 3:16.

13. A friend of mine told me she wondered if Abraham might have had a hunch God would intervene and save Isaac. Good question. I'm not sure.

14. This response is similar to Isaiah's when God spoke to him in Isaiah 6:1-8.

15. See, for example, Isaiah 30:21 and John 14:26.

16. See, for example, Hebrews 4:12.

17. "Ex-NFL star Tillman makes 'ultimate sacrifice.'" April 26, 2004, http://www.msnbc.msn.com/id/4815441/.

18. "Ex-NFL star Tillman makes 'ultimate sacrifice.'"

19. To learn more about the life of Pat Tillman, log on to http://www.pattillmanfoundation.net.

20. Oswald Chambers, *My Utmost for His Highest: Selections for the Year* (Uhrichsville, OH: Barbour, 1997), 120.

Benediction

1. Read Hebrews 11, dubbed the Hall of Faith, to explore more of these courageous men and women of the faith.

2. Michael Yaconelli, *Dangerous Wonder: The Adventure of Childlike Faith* (Colorado Springs, CO: NavPress, 2003), 116.

3. For Jesus' words on rewards in heaven, see, for example, Matthew 5:12; 6:4-6,18; 16:27; Genesis 15:1; Mark 10:21; Psalm 62:12; Ephesians 6:8; 2 Corinthians 5:10; Proverbs 19:17.

4. Also see 1 Corinthians 9:25-27; 2 Timothy 4:7-8.

5. Sir Francis Drake, "Disturb Us, Lord," 1577, http://users3.ev1 .net/~gaillundblad/DisturbusOhLord.htm.

About the Author

J. R. Briggs is the pastor of Pierced Chapel, a vibrant community of faith targeting twentysomethings. He has written for *Discipleship Journal*, *Rev.*, *Group*, and *Relevant*. He loves to hike, camp, travel, ski, blog, read thought-provoking books, and play disc golf and basketball. J. R. spends his free time blogging and performing as Sox the Fox, the mascot for the Colorado Rockies' Triple-A minor league baseball team, the Colorado Springs Sky Sox. Check out his blog at http://brokenstainedglass.typepad.com. He and his wife, Megan, live in Colorado Springs, Colorado.

LEARN TO GET REAL WITH GOD.

Renovation of the Heart: An Interactive Student Edition

Dallas Willard and Randy Frazee

1-57683-730-0

With easy-to-understand examples, review questions, and explanations of keywords, this book will help you understand one of the most complicated and important lessons of life: putting on the character of Christ.

Posers, Fakers, and Wannabes

Brennan Manning and Jim Hancock

1-57683-465-4

Adapted from *Abba's Child* by Brennan Manning, *Posers, Fakers, and Wannabes* will show students how with God's grace, they don't need to put on an act—they can just be real.

Honest to God

Charlie Starr

1-57683-647-9

Examine some of the most important and honest characters in the Bible—Abraham, Jacob, David, Jesus, and others—and learn what they knew about God. Find out why wrestling with the truth can actually bring you closer to Him.

NAVPRESS

BRINGING TRUTH TO LIFE

www.navpress.com

To order copies, visit your local Christian bookstore,
call NavPress at 1-800-366-7788, or log on to www.navpress.com.
To locate a Christian bookstore near you,
call 1-800-991-7747.